R. H. Tawney

THE ACQUISITIVE SOCIETY

◇

A Harvest/HBJ Book
Harcourt Brace Jovanovich, Publishers
San Diego   New York   London

CONTENTS

I	Introductory	1
II	Rights and Functions	8
III	The Acquisitive Society	20
IV	The Nemesis of Industrialism	33
V	Property and Creative Work	52
VI	The Functional Society	84
VII	Industry as a Profession	91
VIII	The "Vicious Circle"	123
IX	The Condition of Efficiency	139
X	The Position of the Brain Worker	161
XI	Porro Unum Necessarium	180
	Index	185

The author desires to express his acknowledgments to the Editor of the *Hibbert Journal* for permission to reprint an article which appeared in it.

ONE

INTRODUCTORY

◆

IT is a commonplace that the characteristic virtue of Englishmen is their power of sustained practical activity, and their characteristic vice a reluctance to test the quality of that activity by reference to principles. They are incurious as to theory, take fundamentals for granted, and are more interested in the state of the roads than in their place on the map. And it might fairly be argued that in ordinary times that combination of intellectual tameness with practical energy is sufficiently serviceable to explain, if not to justify, the equanimity with which its possessors bear the criticism of more mentally adventurous nations. It is the mood of those who have made their bargain with fate and are content to take what it offers without re-opening the deal. It leaves the mind free to concentrate undisturbed upon profitable activities, because it is not distracted by a taste for unprofitable speculations. Most generations, it might be said, walk in a path which they neither make, nor discover, but accept; the main thing is that they should march. The blinkers worn by Englishmen enable them to trot all the more steadily along the beaten road, without being disturbed by curiosity as to their destination.

But if the medicine of the constitution ought not to be made its daily food, neither can its daily food be made its medicine. There are times which are not ordinary, and in such times it is not enough to follow the road. It is necessary to know where it leads, and, if it leads nowhere, to follow another. The search for another involves reflection, which is uncongenial to the bustling people who describe themselves as practical, because they take things as they are and leave them as they are. But the practical thing for a traveler who is uncertain of his path is not to proceed with the utmost rapidity in the wrong direction: it is to consider how to find the right one. And the practical thing for a nation which has stumbled upon one of the turning-points of history is not to behave as though nothing very important were involved, as if it did not matter whether it turned to the right or to the left, went up hill or down dale, provided that it continued doing with a little more energy what it has done hitherto; but to consider whether what it has done hitherto is wise, and, if it is not wise, to alter it. When the broken ends of its industry, its politics, its social organization, have to be pieced together after a catastrophe, it must make a decision; for it makes a decision even if it refuses to decide. If it is to make a decision which will wear, it must travel beyond the philosophy momentarily in favor with the proprietors of its newspapers. Unless it is to move with the energetic futility of a squirrel in a revolving cage, it must have a clear apprehension both of the deficiency of what is, and of the character of what ought to be. And to obtain this apprehension it must appeal to some standard more stable than the momentary exigencies of its commerce or industry or social life, and judge them by it. It must, in short, have recourse to Principles.

Such considerations are, perhaps, not altogether irrelevant at a time when facts have forced upon Englishmen the reconsideration of their social institutions which no appeal to theory could induce them to undertake. An appeal to principles is the condition of any considerable reconstruction of society, because social institutions are the visible expression of the scale of moral values which rules the minds of individuals, and it is impossible to alter institutions without altering that moral valuation. Parliament, industrial organizations, the whole complex machinery through which society expresses itself, is a mill which grinds only what is put into it, and when nothing is put into it grinds air. There are many, of course, who desire no alteration, and who, when it is attempted, will oppose it. They have found the existing economic order profitable in the past. They desire only such changes as will insure that it is equally profitable in the future. *Quand le Roi avait bu, la Pologne était ivre.* They are genuinely unable to understand why their countrymen cannot bask happily by the fire which warms themselves, and ask, like the French farmer-general:—" When everything goes so happily, why trouble to change it ? " Such persons are to be pitied, for they lack the social quality which is proper to man. But they do not need argument; for Heaven has denied them one of the faculties required to apprehend it.

There are others, however, who are conscious of the desire for a new social order, but who yet do not grasp the implications of their own desire. Men may genuinely sympathize with the demand for a radical change. They may be conscious of social evils and sincerely anxious to remove them. They may set up a new department, and appoint new officials, and invent a new name to express their resolution to effect something more drastic than reform, and less disturbing than revolution. But unless they will take the pains, not only to act, but to reflect, they end by effecting nothing. For they deliver themselves bound to those who think they are practical, because they take their philosophy so much for granted as to be unconscious of its implications, and directly they try to act, that philosophy re-asserts itself, and serves as an overruling force which presses their action more deeply into the old channels. "Unhappy man that I am; who shall deliver me from the body of this death?" When they desire to place their economic life on a better foundation, they repeat, like parrots, the word "Productivity," because that is the word that rises first in their minds; regardless of the fact that productivity is the foundation on which it is based already, that increased productivity is the one characteristic achievement of the age before the war, as religion was of the Middle Ages or art of classical Athens, and that it is precisely in the century which has seen the greatest increase in productivity since the fall of the Roman Empire that economic discontent has been most acute. When they are touched by social compunction, they can think of nothing more original than the diminution of poverty, because poverty, being the opposite of the riches which they value most, seems to them the most terrible of human afflictions. They do not understand that poverty is a symptom and a consequence of social disorder, while the disorder itself is something at once more fundamental and more incorrigible, and that the quality in their social life which causes it to demoralize a few by excessive riches, is also the quality which causes it to demoralize many by excessive poverty.

"But increased production is important." Of course it is! That plenty is good and scarcity evil—it needs no ghost from the graves of the past five years to tell us that. But plenty depends upon co-operative effort, and co-operation upon moral principles. And moral principles are what the prophets of this dispensation despise. So the world "continues in scarcity," because it is too grasping and too short-sighted to seek that "which maketh men to be of one mind in a house." The well-intentioned schemes for social reorganization put forward by its commercial teachers are abortive, because they endeavor to combine incompatibles, and, if they disturb everything, settle nothing. They are like a man who, when he finds that his shoddy boots wear badly, orders a pair two sizes larger instead of a pair of good leather, or who makes up for putting a bad sixpence in the plate on Sunday by putting in a bad shilling the next. And when their fit of feverish energy has spent itself, and there is nothing to show for it except disillusionment, they cry that reform is impracticable, and blame human nature, when what they ought to blame is themselves.

Yet all the time the principles upon which industry should be based are simple, however difficult it may be to apply them; and if they are overlooked it is not because they are difficult, but because they are elementary. They are simple because industry is simple. An industry, when all is said, is, in its essence, nothing more mysterious than a body of men associated, in various degrees of competition and co-operation, to win their living by providing the community with some service which it requires. Organize it as you will, let it be a group of craftsmen laboring with hammer and chisel, or peasants plowing their own fields, or armies of mechanics of a hundred different trades constructing ships which are miracles of complexity with machines which are the climax of centuries of invention, its function is service, its method is association. Because its function is service, an industry as a whole has rights and duties towards the community, the abrogation of which involves privilege. Because its method is association, the different parties within it have rights and duties towards each other; and the neglect or perversion of these involves oppression.

The conditions of a right organization of industry are, therefore, permanent, unchanging, and capable of being apprehended by the most elementary intelligence, provided it will read the nature of its countrymen in the large outlines of history, not in the bloodless abstractions of experts. The first is that it should be subordinated to the community in such a way as to render the best service technically possible, that those who render no service should not be paid at all, because it is of the essence of a function that it should find its meaning in the satisfaction, not of itself, but of the end which it serves. The second is that its direction and government should be in the hands of persons who are responsible to those who are directed and governed, because it is the condition of economic freedom that men should not be ruled by an authority which they cannot control. The industrial problem, in fact, is a problem of right, not merely of material misery, and because it is a problem of right it is most acute among those sections of the working classes whose material misery is least. It is a question, first of Function, and secondly of Freedom.

TWO

RIGHTS AND FUNCTIONS

♦

A FUNCTION may be defined as an activity which em-
bodies and expresses the idea of social purpose. The
essence of it is that the agent does not perform it merely
for personal gain or to gratify himself, but recognizes
that he is responsible for its discharge to some higher
authority. The purpose of industry is obvious. It is
to supply man with things which are necessary, useful
or beautiful, and thus to bring life to body or spirit.
In so far as it is governed by this end, it is among the
most important of human activities. In so far as it is
diverted from it, it may be harmless, amusing, or even
exhilarating to those who carry it on, but it possesses
no more social significance than the orderly business of
ants and bees, the strutting of peacocks, or the struggles
of carnivorous animals over carrion.

Men have normally appreciated this fact, however unwilling or unable they may have been to act upon it;
and therefore from time to time, in so far as they have
been able to control the forces of violence and greed,
they have adopted various expedients for emphasizing
the social quality of economic activity. It is not easy,
however, to emphasize it effectively, because to do so
requires a constant effort of will, against which ego-
tistical instincts are in rebellion, and because, if that
will is to prevail, it must be embodied in some social

and political organization, which may itself become so arbitrary, tyrannical and corrupt as to thwart the performance of function instead of promoting it. When this process of degeneration has gone far, as in most European countries it had by the middle of the eighteenth century, the indispensable thing is to break the dead organization up and to clear the ground. In the course of doing so, the individual is emancipated and his rights are enlarged; but the idea of social purpose is discredited by the discredit justly attaching to the obsolete order in which it is embodied.

It is not surprising, therefore, that in the new industrial societies which arose on the ruins of the old régime the dominant note should have been the insistence upon individual rights, irrespective of any social purpose to which their exercise contributed. The economic expansion which concentrated population on the coal-measures was, in essence, an immense movement of colonization drifting from the south and east to the north and west; and it was natural that in those regions of England, as in the American settlements, the characteristic philosophy should be that of the pioneer and the mining camp. The change of social quality was profound. But in England, at least, it was gradual, and the "industrial revolution," though catastrophic in its effects, was only the visible climax of generations of subtle moral change. The rise of modern economic relations, which may be dated in England from the latter half of the seventeenth century, was coincident with the growth of a political theory which replaced the conception of purpose by that of mechanism. During a great part of history men had

found the significance of their social order in its relation to the universal purposes of religion. It stood as
one rung in a ladder which stretched from hell to Paradise, and the classes who composed it were the hands,
the feet, the head of a corporate body which was itself
a microcosm imperfectly reflecting a larger universe.
When the Reformation made the Church a department
of the secular government, it undermined the already en-
feebled spiritual forces which had erected that sublime,
but too much elaborated, synthesis. But its influence
remained for nearly a century after the roots which fed
it had been severed. It was the atmosphere into which
men were born, and from which, however practical, or
even Machiavellian, they could not easily disengage
their spirits. Nor was it inconvenient for the new state-
craft to see the weight of a traditional religious sanction
added to its own concern in the subordination of all
classes and interests to the common end, of which it
conceived itself, and during the greater part of the six-
teenth century was commonly conceived, to be the guardian. The lines of the social structure were no longer
supposed to reproduce in miniature the plan of a universal order. But common habits, common traditions
and beliefs, common pressure from above gave them a
unity of direction, which restrained the forces of individual variation and lateral expansion; and the center
towards which they converged, formerly a Church possessing some of the characteristics of a State, was now a
State that had clothed itself with many of the attributes
of a Church.

The difference between the England of Shakespeare,

still visited by the ghosts of the Middle Ages, and the England which merged in 1700 from the fierce polemics of the last two generations, was a difference of social and political theory even more than of constitutional and political arrangements. Not only the facts, but the minds which appraised them, were profoundly modified. The essence of the change was the disappearance of the idea that social institutions and economic activities were related to common ends, which gave them their significance and which served as their criterion. In the eighteenth century both the State and the Church had abdicated that part of the sphere which had consisted in the maintenance of a common body of social ethics; what was left of it was repression of a class, not the discipline of a nation. Opinion ceased to regard social institutions and economic activity as amenable, like personal conduct, to moral criteria, because it was no longer influenced by the spectacle of institutions which, arbitrary, capricious, and often corrupt in their practical operation, had been the outward symbol and expression of the subordination of life to purposes transcending private interests. That part of government which had been concerned with social administration, if it did not end, became at least obsolescent. For such democracy as had existed in the Middle Ages was dead, and the democracy of the Revolution was not yet born, so that government passed into the lethargic hand of classes who wielded the power of the State in the interests of an irresponsible aristocracy. And the Church was even more remote from the daily life of mankind than the State. Philanthropy abounded; but religion, once the greatest social force, had become a thing as private and individual as the estate of the squire or the working clothes of the laborer.   There were special dispensations and occasional interventions, like the acts of a monarch who reprieved a criminal or signed an order for his execution.   But what was familiar, and human and lovable—what was Christian in Christianity had largely disappeared.   God had been thrust into the frigid altitudes of infinite space.   There was a limited monarchy in Heaven, as well as upon earth.   Providence was the spectator of the curious machine which it had constructed and set in motion, but the operation of which it was neither able nor willing to control.   Like the occasional intervention of the Crown in the proceedings of Parliament, its wisdom was revealed in the infrequency of its interference.

The natural consequence of the abdication of authorities which had stood, however imperfectly, for a common purpose in social organization, was the gradual disappearance from social thought of the idea of purpose itself.   Its place in the eighteenth century was taken by the idea of mechanism.   The conception of men as united to each other, and of all mankind as united to God, by mutual obligations arising from their relation to a common end, which vaguely conceived and imperfectly realized, had been the keystone holding together the social fabric, ceased to be impressed upon men's minds, when Church and State withdrew from the center of social life to its circumference.   What remained when the keystone of the arch was removed, was private rights and private interests, the materials of a society rather

than a society itself. These rights and interests were
the natural order which had been distorted by the ambitions of kings and priests, and which emerged when the
artificial super-structure disappeared, because they were
the creation, not of man, but of Nature herself. They
had been regarded in the past as relative to some public
end, whether religion or national welfare. Henceforward they were thought to be absolute and indefeasible,
and to stand by their own virtue. They were the ultimate political and social reality; and since they were
the ultimate reality, they were not subordinate to other
aspects of society, but other aspects of society were
subordinate to them.

The State could not encroach upon these rights, for
the State existed for their maintenance. They determined the relation of classes, for the most obvious and
fundamental of all rights was property—property absolute and unconditioned—and those who possessed it
were regarded as the natural governors of those who did
not. Society arose from their exercise, through the con-
tracts of individual with individual. It fulfilled its
object in so far as, by maintaining contractual freedom,
it secured full scope for their unfettered exercise. It
failed in so far as, like the French monarchy, it over-
rode them by the use of an arbitrary authority. Thus
conceived, society assumed something of the appearance
of a great joint-stock company, in which political power
and the receipt of dividends were justly assigned to
those who held the most numerous shares. The currents
of social activity did not converge upon common ends,
but were dispersed through a multitude of channels,

created by the private interests of the individuals who composed society. But in their very variety and spontaneity, in the very absence of any attempt to relate them to a larger purpose than that of the individual, lay the best security of its attainment. There is a mysticism of reason as well as of emotion, and the eighteenth century found, in the beneficence of natural instincts, a substitute for the God whom it had expelled from contact with society, and did not hesitate to identify them.

" Thus God and nature planned the general frame
And bade self-love and social be the same."

The result of such ideas in the world of practice was a society which was ruled by law, not by the caprice of Governments, but which recognized no moral limitation on the pursuit by individuals of their economic self-interest. In the world of thought, it was a political philosophy which made rights the foundation of the social order, and which considered the discharge of obligations, when it considered it at all, as emerging by an inevitable process from their free exercise. The first famous exponent of this philosophy was Locke, in whom the dominant conception is the indefeasibility of private rights, not the pre-ordained harmony between private rights and public welfare. In the great French writers who prepared the way for the Revolution, while believing that they were the servants of an enlightened absolutism, there is an almost equal emphasis upon the sanctity of rights and upon the infallibility of the alchemy by which the pursuit of private ends is transmuted into the attainment of public good.   Though their writings reveal the influence of the conception of society as a self-adjusting mechanism, which afterwards became the most characteristic note of the English individualism, what the French Revolution burned into the mind of Europe was the former not the latter.   In England the idea of right had been negative and defensive, a barrier to the encroachment of Governments. The French leapt to the attack from trenches which the English had been content to defend, and in France the idea became affirmative and militant, not a weapon of defense, but a principle of social organization.   The attempt to refound society upon rights, and rights springing not from musty charters, but from the very nature of man himself, was at once the triumph and the limitation of the Revolution.   It gave it the enthusiasm and infectious power of religion.

What happened in England might seem at first sight to have been precisely the reverse.   English practical men, whose thoughts were pitched in a lower key, were a little shocked by the pomp and brilliance of that tremendous creed.   They had scanty sympathy with the absolute affirmations of France.   What captured their imagination was not the right to liberty, which made no appeal to their commercial instincts, but the expediency of liberty, which did; and when the Revolution had revealed the explosive power of the idea of natural right, they sought some less menacing formula.   It had been offered them first by Adam Smith and his precursors, who showed how the mechanism of economic life converted " as with an invisible hand," the exercise of individual rights into the instrument of public good. Bentham, who despised metaphysical subtleties, and thought the Declaration of the Rights of Man as absurd as any other dogmatic religion, completed the new orientation by supplying the final criterion of political institutions in the principle of Utility. Henceforward emphasis was transferred from the right of the individual to exercise his freedom as he pleased to the expediency of an undisturbed exercise of freedom to society.

The change is significant. It is the difference between the universal and equal citizenship of France, with its five million peasant proprietors, and the organized inequality of England established solidly upon class traditions and class institutions; the descent from hope to resignation, from the fire and passion of an age of illimitable vistas to the monotonous beat of the factory engine, from Turgot and Condorcet to the melancholy mathematical creed of Bentham and Ricardo and James Mill. Mankind has, at least, this superiority over its philosophers, that great movements spring from the heart and embody a faith, not the nice adjustments of the hedonistic calculus. So in the name of the rights of property France abolished in three years a great mass of property rights which, under the old régime had robbed the peasant of part of the produce of his labor, and the social transformation survived a whole world of political changes. In England the glad tidings of democracy were broken too discreetly to reach the ears of the hind in the furrow or the shepherd on the hill:

there were political changes without a social transformation. The doctrine of Utility, though trenchant in the sphere of politics, involved no considerable interference with the fundamentals of the social fabric. Its exponents were principally concerned with the removal of political abuses and legal anomalies. They attacked sinecures and pensions and the criminal code and the procedure of the law courts. But they touched only the surface of social institutions. They thought it a monstrous injustice that the citizen should pay one-tenth of his income in taxation to an idle Government, but quite reasonable that he should pay one-fifth of it in rent to an idle landlord.

The difference, neverthelesss, was one of emphasis and expression, not of principle. It mattered very little in practice whether private property and unfettered economic freedom were stated, as in France, to be natural rights, or whether, as in England, they were merely assumed once for all to be expedient. In either case they were taken for granted as the fundamentals upon which social organization was to be based, and about which no further argument was admissible. Though Bentham argued that rights were derived from utility, not from nature, he did not push his analysis so far as to argue that any particular right was relative to any particular function, and thus endorsed indiscriminately rights which were not accompanied by service as well as rights which were. While eschewing, in short, the phraseology of natural rights, the English Utilitarians retained something not unlike the substance of them. For they assumed that private property in land, and the private ownership of capital, were natural institutions, and gave them, indeed, a new lease of life, by proving to their own satisfaction that social well-being must result from their continued exercise. Their negative was as important as their positive teaching. It was a conductor which diverted the lightning. Behind their political theory, behind the practical conduct, which as always, continues to express theory long after it has been discredited in the world of thought, lay the acceptance of absolute rights to property and to economic freedom as the unquestioned center of social organization.

The result of that attitude was momentous. The motive and inspiration of the Liberal Movement of the eighteenth century had been the attack on Privilege. But the creed which had exorcised the specter of agrarian feudalism haunting village and *château* in France, was impotent to disarm the new ogre of industrialism which was stretching its limbs in the north of England. When, shorn of its splendors and illusions, liberalism triumphed in England in 1832, it carried without criticism into the new world of capitalist industry categories of private property and freedom of contract which had been forged in the simpler economic environment of the pre-industrial era. In England these categories are being bent and twisted till they are no longer recognizable, and will, in time, be made harmless. In America, where necessity compelled the crystallization of principles in a constitution, they have the rigidity of an iron jacket. The magnificent formulæ in which a society of farmers and master craftsmen enshrined its philosophy of freedom are in danger of becoming fetters used by an Anglo-Saxon business aristocracy to bind insurgent movements on the part of an immigrant and semi-servile proletariat.

THREE

THE ACQUISITIVE SOCIETY

♦

THIS doctrine has been qualified in practice by particular limitations to avert particular evils and to meet exceptional emergencies. But it is limited in special cases precisely because its general validity is regarded as beyond controversy, and, up to the eve of the present war, it was the working faith of modern economic civilization. What it implies is, that the foundation of society is found, not in functions, but in rights; that rights are not deducible from the discharge of functions, so that the acquisition of wealth and the enjoyment of property are contingent upon the performances of services, but that the individual enters the world equipped with rights to the free disposal of his property and the pursuit of his economic self-interest, and that these rights are anterior to, and independent of, any service which he may render. True, the service of society will, in fact, it is assumed, result from their exercise. But it is not the primary motive and criterion of industry, but a secondary consequence, which emerges incidentally through the exercise of rights, a consequence which is attained, indeed, in practice, but which is attained without being sought. It is not the end at which economic activity aims, or the standard by which it is judged, but a by-product, as coal-tar is a by-product of the manu-

facture of gas; whether that by-product appears or
not, it is not proposed that the rights themselves should
be abdicated. For they are regarded, not as a conditional trust, but as a property, which may, indeed,
give way to the special exigencies of extraordinary
emergencies, but which resumes its sway when the
emergency is over, and in normal times is above discussion.

That conception is written large over the history
of the nineteenth century, both in England and in
America. The doctrine which it inherited was that
property was held by an absolute right on an individual basis, and to this fundamental it added another, which can be traced in principle far back into
history, but which grew to its full stature only after
the rise of capitalist industry, that societies act both
unfairly and unwisely when they limit opportunities
of economic enterprise. Hence every attempt to impose obligations as a condition of the tenure of property or of the exercise of economic activity has been
met by uncompromising resistance. The story of the
struggle between humanitarian sentiment and the theory of property transmitted from the eighteenth century is familiar. No one has forgotten the opposition offered in the name of the rights of property to
factory legislation, to housing reform, to interference
with the adulteration of goods, even to the compulsory
sanitation of private houses. "May I not do what I
like with my own?" was the answer to the proposal
to require a minimum standard of safety and sanitation from the owners of mills and houses. Even to

this day, while an English urban landlord can cramp
or distort the development of a whole city by with-
holding land except at fancy prices, English municipalities are without adequate powers of compulsory
purchase, and must either pay through the nose or
see thousands of their members overcrowded.   The
whole body of procedure by which they may acquire
land, or indeed new powers of any kind, has been
carefully designed by lawyers to protect owners of
property against the possibility that their private
rights may be subordinated to the public interest,
because their rights are thought to be primary
and absolute and public interests secondary and
contingent.

No one needs to be reminded, again, of the influence
of the same doctrine in the sphere of taxation.   Thus
the income tax was excused as a temporary measure,
because the normal society was conceived to be one
in which the individual spent his whole income for
himself and owed no obligations to society on account
of it.   The death duties were denounced as robbery,
because they implied that the right to benefit by inheritance was conditional upon a social sanction.   The
Budget of 1909 created a storm, not because the taxation of land was heavy—in amount the land-taxes were
trifling—but because it was felt to involve the doctrine that property is not an absolute right, but that
it may properly be accompanied by special obligations,
a doctrine which, if carried to its logical conclusion,
would destroy its sanctity by making ownership no
longer absolute but conditional.

Such an implication seems intolerable to an influential body of public opinion, because it has been accustomed to regard the free disposal of property and the unlimited exploitation of economic opportunities, as rights which are absolute and unconditioned. On the whole, until recently, this opinion had few antagonists who could not be ignored. As a consequence the maintenance of property rights has not been seriously threatened even in those cases in which it is evident that no service is discharged, directly or indirectly, by their exercise. No one supposes, that the owner of urban land, performs *qua* owner, any function. He has a right of private taxation; that is all. But the private ownership of urban land is as secure to-day as it was a century ago; and Lord Hugh Cecil, in his interesting little book on Conservatism, declares that whether private property is mischievous or not, society cannot interfere with it, because to interfere with it is theft, and theft is wicked. No one supposes that it is for the public good that large areas of land should be used for parks and game. But our country gentlemen are still settled heavily upon their villages and still slay their thousands. No one can argue that a monopolist is impelled by " an invisible hand " to serve the public interest. But over a considerable field of industry competition, as the recent Report on Trusts shows, has been replaced by combination, and combinations are allowed the same unfettered freedom as individuals in the exploitation of economic opportunities. No one really believes that the production of coal depends upon the payment of mining royalties or that ships will not go to and fro unless ship-owners can earn fifty per cent. upon their capital. But coal mines, or rather the coal miner, still pay royalties, and ship-owners still make fortunes and are made Peers.

At the very moment when everybody is talking about the importance of increasing the output of wealth, the last question, apparently, which it occurs to any statesman to ask is why wealth should be squandered on futile activities, and in expenditure which is either disproportionate to service or made for no service at all. So inveterate, indeed, has become the practice of payment in virtue of property rights, without even the pretense of any service being rendered, that when, in a national emergency, it is proposed to extract oil from the ground, the Government actually proposes that every gallon shall pay a tax to landowners who never even suspected its existence, and the ingenuous proprietors are full of pained astonishment at any one questioning whether the nation is under moral obligation to endow them further. Such rights are, strictly speaking, privileges. For the definition of a privilege is a right to which no corresponding function is attached.

The enjoyment of property and the direction of industry are considered, in short, to require no social justification, because they are regarded as rights which stand by their own virtue, not functions to be judged by the success with which they contribute to a social purpose. To-day that doctrine, if intellectually discredited, is still the practical foundation of social organization. How slowly it yields even to the most insistent demonstration of its inadequacy is shown by the attitude which the heads of the business world have adopted to the restrictions imposed on economic activity during the war. The control of railways, mines and shipping, the distribution of raw materials through a public department instead of through competing merchants, the regulation of prices, the attempts to check "profiteering"—the detailed application of these measures may have been effective or ineffective, wise or injudicious. It is evident, indeed, that some of them have been foolish, like the restriction of imports when the world has five years' destruction to repair, and that others, if sound in conception, have been questionable in their execution. If they were attacked on the ground that they obstruct the efficient performance of function—if the leaders of industry came forward and said generally, as some, to their honor, have:—"We accept your policy, but we will improve its execution; we desire payment for service and service only and will help the state to see that it pays for nothing else"—there might be controversy as to the facts, but there could be none as to the principle.

In reality, however, the gravamen of the charges brought against these restrictions appears generally to be precisely the opposite. They are denounced by most of their critics not because they limit the opportunity of service, but because they diminish the opportunity for gain, not because they prevent the trader enriching the community, but because they make it more difficult for him to enrich himself; not, in short, because they have failed to convert economic activity into a social function, but because they have come too near succeeding. If the financial adviser to the Coal Controller may be trusted, the shareholders in coal mines would appear to have done fairly well during the war. But the proposal to limit their profits to 1/2 per ton is described by Lord Gainford as " sheer robbery and confiscation." With some honorable exceptions, what is demanded is that in the future as in the past the directors of industry should be free to handle it as an enterprise conducted for their own convenience or advancement, instead of being compelled, as they have been partially compelled during the war, to subordinate it to a social purpose. For to admit that the criterion of commerce and industry is its success in discharging a social purpose is at once to turn property and economic activity from rights which are absolute into rights which are contingent and derivative, because it is to affirm that they are relative to functions and that they may justly be revoked when the functions are not performed. It is, in short, to imply that property and economic activity exist to promote the ends of society, whereas hitherto society has been regarded in the world of business as existing to promote them. To those who hold their position, not as functionaries, but by virtue of their success in making industry contribute to their own wealth and social influence, such a reversal of means and ends appears little less than a revolution. For it means that they must justify before a social tribunal rights which they have hitherto taken for granted as part of an order which is above criticism.

During the greater part of the nineteenth century the significance of the opposition between the two principles of individual rights and social functions was masked by the doctrine of the inevitable harmony between private interests and public good. Competition, it was argued, was an effective substitute for honesty. To-day that subsidiary doctrine has fallen to pieces under criticism; few now would profess adherence to the compound of economic optimism and moral bankruptcy which led a nineteenth century economist to say: "Greed is held in check by greed, and the desire for gain sets limits to itself." The disposition to regard individual rights as the center and pivot of society is still, however, the most powerful element in political thought and the practical foundation of industrial organization. The laborious refutation of the doctrine that private and public interests are coincident, and that man's self-love is God's Providence, which was the excuse of the last century for its worship of economic egotism, has achieved, in fact, surprisingly small results. Economic egotism is still worshiped; and it is worshiped because that doctrine was not really the center of the position. It was an outwork, not the citadel, and now that the outwork has been captured, the citadel is still to win.

What gives its special quality and character, its toughness and cohesion, to the industrial system built up in the last century and a half, is not its exploded theory of economic harmonies. It is the doctrine that economic rights are anterior to, and independent of economic functions, that they stand by their own virtue, and need adduce no higher credentials. The practical result of it is that economic rights remain, whether economic functions are performed or not. They remain to-day in a more menacing form than in the age of early industrialism. For those who control industry no longer compete but combine, and the rivalry between property in capital and property in land has long since ended. The basis of the New Conservatism appears to be a determination so to organize society, both by political and economic action, as to make it secure against every attempt to extinguish payments which are made, not for service, but because the owners possess a right to extract income without it. Hence the fusion of the two traditional parties, the proposed "strengthening" of the second chamber, the return to protection, the swift conversion of rival industrialists to the advantages of monopoly, and the attempts to buy off with concessions the more influential section of the working classes. Revolutions, as a long and bitter experience reveals, are apt to take their color from the régime which they overthrow. Is it any wonder that the creed which affirms the absolute rights of property should sometimes be met with a counter-affirmation of the absolute rights of labor, less anti-social, indeed, and inhuman, but almomst as dogmatic, almost as intolerant and thoughtless as itself?

A society which aimed at making the acquisition of wealth contingent upon the discharge of social obligations, which sought to proportion remuneration to service and denied it to those by whom no service was performed, which inquired first not what men possess but what they can make or create or achieve, might be called a Functional Society, because in such a society the main subject of social emphasis would be the performance of functions. But such a society does not exist, even as a remote ideal, in the modern world, though something like it has hung, an unrealized theory, before men's minds in the past. Modern societies aim at protecting economic rights, while leaving economic functions, except in moments of abnormal emergency, to fulfil themselves. The motive which gives color and quality to their public institutions, to their policy and political thought, is not the attempt to secure the fulfilment of tasks undertaken for the public service, but to increase the opportunities open to individuals of attaining the objects which they conceive to be advantageous to themselves. If asked the end or criterion of social organization, they would give an answer reminiscent of the formula the greatest happiness of the greatest number. But to say that the end of social institutions is happiness, is to say that they have no common end at all. For happiness is individual, and to make happiness the object of society is to resolve society itself into the ambitions of numberless individuals, each directed towards the attainment of some personal purpose.

Such societies may be called Acquisitive Societies, because their whole tendency and interest and preoccupation is to promote the acquisition of wealth. The appeal of this conception must be powerful, for it has laid the whole modern world under its spell.   Since England first revealed the possibilities of industrialism, it has gone from strength to strength, and as industrial civilization invades countries hitherto remote from it, as Russia and Japan and India and China are drawn into its orbit, each decade sees a fresh extension of its influence.   The secret of its triumph is obvious.   It is an invitation to men to use the powers with which they have been endowed by nature or society, by skill or energy or relentless egotism or mere good fortune, without inquiring whether there is any principle by which their exercise should be limited. It assumes the social organization which determines the opportunities which different classes shall in fact possess, and concentrates attention upon the right of those who possess or can acquire power to make the fullest use of it for their own self-advancement.   By fixing men's minds, not upon the discharge of social obligations, which restricts their energy, because it defines the goal to which it should be directed, but upon the exercise of the right to pursue their own self-interest, it offers unlimited scope for the acquisition of riches, and therefore gives free play to one of the most powerful of human instincts.   To the strong it promises unfettered freedom for the exercise of their strength; to the weak the hope that they too one day may be strong.   Before the eyes of both it suspends a golden prize, which not all can attain, but for which each may strive, the enchanting vision of infinite expansion.   It assures men that there are no ends other than their ends, no law other than their desires, no limit other than that which they think advisable. Thus it makes the individual the center of his own universe, and dissolves moral principles into a choice of expediences. And it immensely simplifies the problems of social life in complex communities. For it relieves them of the necessity of discriminating between different types of economic activity and different sources of wealth, between enterprise and avarice, energy and unscrupulous greed, property which is legitimate and property which is theft, the just enjoyment of the fruits of labor and the idle parasitism of birth or fortune, because it treats all economic activities as standing upon the same level, and suggests that excess or defect, waste or superfluity, require no conscious effort of the social will to avert them, but are corrected almost automatically by the mechanical play of economic forces.

Under the impulse of such ideas men do not become religious or wise or artistic; for religion and wisdom and art imply the acceptance of limitations. But they become powerful and rich. They inherit the earth and change the face of nature, if they do not possess their own souls; and they have that appearance of freedom which consists in the absence of obstacles between opportunities for self-advancement and those whom birth or wealth or talent or good fortune has placed in a position to seize them. It is not difficult either for individuals or for societies to achieve their object, if that object be sufficiently limited and immediate, and if they are not distracted from its pursuit by other considerations. The temper which dedicates itself to the cultivation of opportunities, and leaves obligations to take care of themselves, is set upon an object which is at once simple and practicable. The eighteenth century defined it. The twentieth century has very largely attained it. Or, if it has not attained it, it has at least grasped the possibilities of its attainment. The national output of wealth per head of population is estimated to have been approximately £40 in 1914. Unless mankind chooses to continue the sacrifice of prosperity to the ambitions and terrors of nationalism, it is possible that by the year 2000 it may be doubled.

FOUR

THE NEMESIS OF INDUSTRIALISM

♦

Such happiness is not remote from achievement. In the course of achieving it, however, the world has been confronted by a group of unexpected consequences, which are the cause of its *malaise,* as the obstruction of economic opportunity was the cause of social *malaise* in the eighteenth century. And these consequences are not, as is often suggested, accidental mal-adjustments, but flow naturally from its dominant principle: so that there is a sense in which the cause of its perplexity is not its failure, but the quality of its success, and its light itself a kind of darkness. The will to economic power, if it is sufficiently single-minded, brings riches. But if it is single-minded it destroys the moral restraints which ought to condition the pursuit of riches, and therefore also makes the pursuit of riches meaningless. For what gives meaning to economic activity, as to any other activity is, as we have said, the purpose to which it is directed. But the faith upon which our economic civilization reposes, the faith that riches are not a means but an end, implies that all economic activity is equally estimable, whether it is subordinated to a social purpose or not. Hence it divorces gain from service, and justifies rewards for which no function is performed, or which are out of all proportion to it. Wealth in modern societies is distributed according to opportunity; and while opportunity depends partly upon talent and energy, it depends still more upon birth, social position, access to education and inherited wealth; in a word, upon property. For talent and energy can create opportunity. But property need only wait for it. It is the sleeping partner who draws the dividends which the firm produces, the residuary legatee who always claims his share in the estate.

Because rewards are divorced from services, so that what is prized most is not riches obtained in return for labor but riches the economic origin of which, being regarded as sordid, is concealed, two results follow. The first is the creation of a class of pensioners upon industry, who levy toll upon its product, but contribute nothing to its increase, and who are not merely tolerated, but applauded and admired and protected with assiduous care, as though the secret of prosperity resided in them. They are admired because in the absence of any principle of discrimination between incomes which are payment for functions and incomes which are not, all incomes, merely because they represent wealth, stand on the same level of appreciation, and are estimated solely by their magnitude, so that in all societies which have accepted industrialism there is an upper layer which claims the enjoyment of social life, while it repudiates its responsibilities. The *rentier* and his ways, how familiar they were in England before the war! A public school and then club life in Oxford and Cambridge, and then another club in town; London in June, when London is pleasant, the moors in August, and pheasants in October, Cannes in

December and hunting in February and March; and a whole world of rising bourgeoisie eager to imitate them, sedulous to make their expensive watches keep time with this preposterous calendar!

The second consequence is the degradation of those who labor, but who do not by their labor command large rewards; that is of the great majority of mankind. And this degradation follows inevitably from the refusal of men to give the purpose of industry the first place in their thought about it. When they do that, when their minds are set upon the fact that the meaning of industry is the service of man, all who labor appear to them honorable, because all who labor serve, and the distinction which separates those who serve from those who merely spend is so crucial and fundamental as to obliterate all minor distinctions based on differences of income. But when the criterion of function is forgotten, the only criterion which remains is that of wealth, and an Acquisitive Society reverences the possession of wealth, as a Functional Society would honor, even in the person of the humblest and most laborious craftsman, the arts of creation.

So wealth becomes the foundation of public esteem, and the mass of men who labor, but who do not acquire wealth, are thought to be vulgar and meaningless and insignificant compared with the few who acquire wealth by good fortune, or by the skilful use of economic opportunities. They come to be regarded, not as the ends for which alone it is worth while to produce wealth at all, but as the instruments of its

acquisition by a world that declines to be soiled by contact with what is thought to be the dull and sordid
business of labor. They are not happy, for the reward
of all but the very mean is not merely money, but the
esteem of their fellow-men, and they know they are not
esteemed, as soldiers, for example, are esteemed, though
it is because they give their lives to making civilization that there is a civilization which it is worth while
for soldiers to defend. They are not esteemed, because the admiration of society is directed towards
those who get, not towards those who give; and though
workmen give much they get little. And the *rentiers*
whom they support are not happy; for in discarding
the idea of function, which sets a limit to the acquisition of riches, they have also discarded the principle
which alone give riches their meaning. Hence unless
they can persuade themselves that to be rich is in itself meritorious, they may bask in social admiration,
but they are unable to esteem themselves. For they
have abolished the principle which makes activity significant, and therefore estimable. They are, indeed,
more truly pitiable than some of those who envy them.
For like the spirits in the Inferno, they are punished
by the attainment of their desires.

A society ruled by these notions is necessarily the
victim of an irrational inequality. To escape such inequality it is necessary to recognize that there is some
principle which ought to limit the gains of particular
classes and particular individuals, because gains drawn
from certain sources or exceeding certain amounts are
illegitimate. But such a limitation implies a stand-

ard of discrimination, which is inconsistent with the
assumption that each man has a right to what he can
get, irrespective of any service rendered for it. Thus
privilege, which was to have been exorcised by the gospel of 1789, returns in a new guise, the creature no
longer of unequal legal rights thwarting the natural
exercise of equal powers of hand and brain, but of
unequal powers springing from the exercise of equal
rights in a world where property and inherited wealth
and the apparatus of class institutions have made opportunities unequal. Inequality, again, leads to the
mis-direction of production. For, since the demand of
one income of £50,000 is as powerful a magnet as the
demand of 500 incomes of £100, it diverts energy from
the creation of wealth to the multiplication of luxuries,
so that, for example, while one-tenth of the people of
England are overcrowded, a considerable part of them
are engaged, not in supplying that deficiency, but in
making rich men's hotels, luxurious yachts, and motor-
cars like that used by the Secretary of State for War,
" with an interior inlaid with silver in quartered ma-
hogany, and upholstered in fawn suede and morocco,"
which was recently bought by a suburban capitalist, by
way of encouraging useful industries and rebuking public extravagance with an example of private economy,
for the trifling sum of 3,550 guineas.

Thus part of the goods which are annually produced,
and which are called wealth, is, strictly speaking, waste,
because it consists of articles which, though reckoned
as part of the income of the nation, either should not
have been produced until other articles had already

been produced in sufficient abundance, or should not have been produced at all. And some part of the population is employed in making goods which no man can make with happiness, or indeed without loss of self-respect, because he knows that they had much better not be made, and that his life is wasted in making them. Everybody recognizes that the army contractor who, in time of war, set several hundred navvies to dig an artificial lake in his grounds, was not adding to, but subtracting from, the wealth of the nation. But in time of peace many hundred thousand workmen, if they are not digging ponds, are doing work which is equally foolish and wasteful; though, in peace, as in war, there is important work, which is waiting to be done, and which is neglected. It is neglected because, while the effective demand of the mass of men is only too small, there is a small class which wears several men's clothes, eats several men's dinners, occupies several families' houses, and lives several men's lives. As long as a minority has so large an income that part of it, if spent at all, must be spent on trivialties, so long will part of the human energy and mechanical equipment of the nation be diverted from serious work, which enriches it, to making trivialities, which impoverishes it, since they can only be made at the cost of not making other things. And if the peers and millionaires who are now preaching the duty of production to miners and dock laborers desire that more wealth, not more waste, should be produced, the simplest way in which they can achieve their aim is to transfer to the public their whole incomes over (say) £1,000 a year, in order that it may be spent in setting to work, not gardeners, chauffeurs, domestic servants and shopkeepers in the West End of London, but builders, mechanics and teachers.

So to those who clamor, as many now do, " Produce! Produce! " one simple question may be addressed:— " Produce what? " Food, clothing, house-room, art, knowledge? By all means! But if the nation is scantily furnished with these things had it not better stop producing a good many others which fill shop windows in Regent Street? If it desires to re-equip its industries with machinery and its railways with wagons, had it not better refrain from holding ex· hibitions designed to encourage rich men to re-equip themselves with motor-cars? What can be more child· ish than to urge the necessity that productive power should be increased, if part of the productive power which exists already is misapplied? Is not *less* production of futilities as important as, indeed a condition of, *more* production of things of moment? Would not " Spend less on private luxuries " be as wise a cry as " produce more " ? Yet this result of inequality, again, is a phenomenon which cannot be prevented, or checked, or even recognized by a society which excludes the idea of purpose from its social arrangements and industrial activity. For to recognize it is to admit that there is a principle superior to the mechanical play of economic forces, which ought to determine the relative importance of different occupations, and thus to abandon the view that all riches, however composed, are an end, and that all economic activity is equally justifiable.

The rejection of the idea of purpose involves another consequence which every one laments, but which no one can prevent, except by abandoning the belief that the free exercise of rights is the main interest of society and the discharge of obligations a secondary and incidental consequence which may be left to take care of itself. It is that social life is turned into a scene of fierce antagonisms and that a considerable part of industry is carried on in the intervals of a disguised social war. The idea that industrial peace can be secured merely by the exercise of tact and forbearance is based on the idea that there is a fundamental identity of interest between the different groups engaged in it, which is occasionally interrupted by regrettable misunderstandings. Both the one idea and the other are an illusion. The disputes which matter are not caused by a misunderstanding of identity of interests, but by a better understanding of diversity of interests. Though a formal declaration of war is an episode, the conditions which issue in a declaration of war are permanent; and what makes them permanent is the conception of industry which also makes inequality and functionless incomes permanent. It is the denial that industry has any end or purpose other than the satisfaction of those engaged in it.

That motive produces industrial warfare, not as a regrettable incident, but as an inevitable result. It produces industrial war, because its teaching is that each individual or group has a right to what they can get, and denies that there is any principle, other than the mechanism of the market, which determines what they ought to get. For, since the income available for distribution is limited, and since, therefore, when certain limits have been passed, what one group gains another group must lose, it is evident that if the relative incomes of different groups are not to be determined by their functions, there is no method other than mutual self-assertion which is left to determine them. Self-interest, indeed, may cause them to refrain from using their full strength to enforce their claims, and, in so far as this happens, peace is secured in industry, as men have attempted to secure it in international affairs, by a balance of power. But the maintenance of such a peace is contingent upon the estimate of the parties to it that they have more to lose than to gain by an overt struggle, and is not the result of their acceptance of any standard of remuneration as an equitable settlement of their claims. Hence it is precarious, insincere and short. It is without finality, because there can be no finality in the mere addition of increments of income, any more than in the gratification of any other desire for material goods. When demands are conceded the old struggle recommences upon a new level, and will always recommence as long as men seek to end it merely by increasing remuneration, not by finding a principle upon which all remuneration, whether large or small, should be based.

Such a principle is offered by the idea of function, because its application would eliminate the surpluses which are the subject of contention, and would make it evident that remuneration is based upon service, not upon chance or privilege or the power to use opportunities to drive a hard bargain. But the idea of function is incompatible with the doctrine that every person and organization have an unlimited right to exploit their economic opportunities as fully as they please, which is the working faith of modern industry; and, since it is not accepted, men resign themselves to the settlement of the issue by force, or propose that the State should supersede the force of private associations by the use of its force, as though the absence of a principle could be compensated by a new kind of machinery. Yet all the time the true cause of industrial warfare is as simple as the true cause of international warfare. It is that if men recognize no law superior to their desires, then they must fight when their desires collide. For though groups or nations which are at issue with each other may be willing to submit to a principle which is superior to them both, there is no reason why they should submit to each other.

Hence the idea, which is popular with rich men, that industrial disputes would disappear if only the output of wealth were doubled, and every one were twice as well off, not only is refuted by all practical experience, but is in its very nature founded upon an illusion. For the question is one not of amounts but of proportions; and men will fight to be paid £30 a week, instead of £20, as readily as they will fight to be paid £5 instead of £4, as long as there is no reason why they should be paid £20 instead of £30, and as long as other men who do not work are paid anything

at all. If miners demanded higher wages when every
superfluous charge upon coal-getting had been eliminated, there would be a principle with which to meet
their claim, the principle that one group of workers
ought not to encroach upon the livelihood of others.
But as long as mineral owners extract royalties, and
exceptionally productive mines pay thirty per cent. to
absentee shareholders, there is no valid answer to a demand for higher wages. For if the community pays
anything at all to those who do not work, it can afford
to pay more to those who do. The naïve complaint, that
workmen are never satisfied, is, therefore, strictly true.
It is true, not only of workmen, but of all classes in
a society which conducts its affairs on the principle
that wealth, instead of being proportioned to function, belongs to those who can get it. They are never
satisfied, nor can they be satisfied. For as long as
they make that principle the guide of their individual
lives and of their social order, nothing short of infinity could bring them satisfaction.

So here, again, the prevalent insistence upon rights,
and prevalent neglect of functions, brings men into
a vicious circle which they cannot escape, without es-
caping from the false philosophy which dominates them.
But it does something more. It makes that philosophy
itself seem plausible and exhilarating, and a rule not
only for industry, in which it had its birth, but for
politics and culture and religion and the whole com-
pass of social life. The possibility that one aspect of
human life may be so exaggerated as to overshadow.

and in time to atrophy, every other, has been made
familiar to Englishmen by the example of " Prussian
militarism." Militarism is the characteristic, not of
an army, but of a society. Its essence is not any particular quality or scale of military preparation, but
a state of mind, which, in its concentration on one particular element in social life, ends finally by exalting
it until it becomes the arbiter of all the rest. The
purpose for which military forces exist is forgotten.
They are thought to stand by their own right and
to need no justification. Instead of being regarded
as an instrument which is necessary in an imperfect
world, they are elevated into an object of superstitious
veneration, as though the world would be a poor in-
sipid place without them, so that political institutions
and social arrangements and intellect and morality and
religion are crushed into a mold made to fit one activity,
which in a sane society is a subordinate activity, like
the police, or the maintenance of prisons, or the cleans-
ing of sewers, but which in a militarist state is a kind
of mystical epitome of society itself.

Militarism, as Englishmen see plainly enough, is
fetich worship. It is the prostration of men's souls
before, and the laceration of their bodies to appease,
an idol. What they do not see is that their reverence
for economic activity and industry and what is called
business is also fetich worship, and that in their devotion to that idol they torture themselves as needlessly
and indulge in the same meaningless antics as the Prussians did in their worship of militarism. For what
the military tradition and spirit have done for Prus-

sia, with the result of creating militarism, the commercial tradition and spirit have done for England, with the result of creating industrialism. Industrialism is no more a necessary characteristic of an economically developed society than militarism is a necessary characteristic of a nation which maintains military forces. It is no more the result of applying science to industry than militarism is the result of the application of science to war, and the idea that it is something inevitable in a community which uses coal and iron and machinery, so far from being the truth, is itself a product of the perversion of mind which industrialism produces. Men may use what mechanical instruments they please and be none the worse for their use. What kills their souls is when they allow their instruments to use *them*. The essence of industrialism, in short, is not any particular method of industry, but a particular estimate of the importance of industry, which results in it being thought the only thing that is important at all, so that it is elevated from the subordinate place which it should occupy among human interests and activities into being the standard by which all other interests and activities are judged.

When a Cabinet Minister declares that the greatness of this country depends upon the volume of its exports, so that France, with exports comparatively little, and Elizabethan England, which exported next to nothing, are presumably to be pitied as altogether inferior civilizations, that is Industrialism. It is the confusion of one minor department of life with the

whole of life. When manufacturers cry and cut themselves with knives, because it is proposed that boys and
girls of fourteen shall attend school for eight hours a
week, and the President of the Board of Education is
so gravely impressed by their apprehensions, that he
at once allows the hours to be reduced to seven, that
is Industrialism. It is fetich worship. When the Government obtains money for a war, which costs £7,000,-
000 a day, by closing the Museums, which cost £20,-
000 a year, that is Industrialism. It is a contempt
for all interests which do not contribute obviously
to economic activity. When the Press clamors that
the one thing needed to make this island an Arcadia
is productivity, and more productivity, and yet more
productivity, that is Industrialism. It is the confusion
of means with ends.

Men will always confuse means with ends if they
are without any clear conception that it is the ends,
not the means, which matter—if they allow their minds
to slip from the fact that it is the social purpose of
industry which gives it meaning and makes it worth
while to carry it on at all. And when they do that,
they will turn their whole world upside down, because
they do not see the poles upon which it ought to move.
So when, like England, they are thoroughly industrialized, they behave like Germany, which was thoroughly
militarized. They talk as though man existed for industry, instead of industry existing for man, as the
Prussians talked of man existing for war. They re-
sent any activity which is not colored by the predom-
inant interest, because it seems a rival to it. So they

destroy religion and art and morality, which cannot exist unless they are disinterested; and having destroyed these, which are the end, for the sake of industry, which is a means, they make their industry itself what they make their cities, a desert of unnatural dreariness, which only forgetfulness can make endurable, and which only excitement can enable them to forget.

Torn by suspicions and recriminations, avid of power, and oblivious of duties, desiring peace, but unable to " seek peace and ensue it," because unwilling to surrender the creed which is the cause of war, to what can one compare such a society but to the international world, which also has been called a society and which also is social in nothing but name? And the comparison is more than a play upon words. It is an analogy which has its roots in the facts of history. It is not a chance that the last two centuries, which saw the new growth of a new system of industry, saw also the growth of the system of international politics which came to a climax in the period from 1870 to 1914. Both the one and the other are the expression of the same spirit and move in obedience to similar laws. The essence of the former was the repudiation of any authority superior to the individual reason. It left men free to follow their own interests or ambitions or appetites, untrammeled by subordination to any common center of allegiance. The essence of the latter was the repudiation of any authority superior to the sovereign state, which again was conceived as a compact self-contained unit—a unit which would lose its very essence if it lost its independence of other states. Just as the one emancipated economic activity from a mesh of antiquated traditions, so the other emancipated nations from arbitrary subordination to alien races or Governments, and turned them into nationalities with a right to work out their own destiny.

Nationalism is, in fact, the counterpart among nations of what individualism is within them. It has similar origins and tendencies, similar triumphs and defects. For nationalism, like individualism, lays its emphasis on the rights of separate units, not on their subordination to common obligations, though its units are races or nations, not individual men. Like individualism it appeals to the self-assertive instincts, to which it promises opportunities of unlimited expansion. Like individualism it is a force of immense explosive power, the just claims of which must be conceded before it is possible to invoke any alternative principle to control its operations. For one cannot impose a supernational authority upon irritated or discontented or oppressed nationalities any more than one can subordinate economic motives to the control of society, until society has recognized that there is a sphere which they may legitimately occupy. And, like individualism, if pushed to its logical conclusion, it is self-destructive. For as nationalism, in its brilliant youth, begins as a claim that nations, because they are spiritual beings, shall determine themselves, and passes too often into a claim that they shall dominate others, so individualism begins by asserting the right of men to make of their own lives what they can, and ends by condoning the subjection of the majority of men to the few whom good fortune or special opportunity or privilege have enabled most successfully to use their rights. They rose together. It is probable that, if ever they decline, they will decline together. For life cannot be cut in compartments. In the long run the world reaps in war what it sows in peace. And to expect that international rivalry can be exorcised as long as the industrial order within each nation is such as to give success to those whose existence is a struggle for self-aggrandizement is a dream which has not even the merit of being beautiful.

So the perversion of nationalism is imperialism, as the perversion of individualism is industrialism. And the perversion comes, not through any flaw or vice in human nature, but by the force of the idea, because the principle is defective and reveals its defects as it reveals its power. For it asserts that the rights of nations and individuals are absolute, which is false, instead of asserting that they are absolute in their own sphere, but that their sphere itself is contingent upon the part which they play in the community of nations and individuals, which is true. Thus it constrains them to a career of indefinite expansion, in which they devour continents and oceans, law, morality and religion, and last of all their own souls, in an attempt to attain infinity by the addition to themselves of all that is finite. In the meantime their rivals, and their subjects, and they themselves are conscious of the danger of opposing forces, and seek to purchase security and to avoid a collision by organizing a balance of power. But the balance, whether in international politics or in industry, is unstable, because it reposes not on the common recognition of a principle by which the claims of nations and individuals are limited, but on an attempt to find an equipoise which may avoid a conflict without adjuring the assertion of unlimited claims. No such equipoise can be found, because, in a world where the possibilities of increasing military or industrial power are illimitable, no such equipoise can exist.

Thus, as long as men move on this plane, there is no solution. They can obtain peace only by surrendering the claim to the unfettered exercise of their rights, which is the cause of war. What we have been witnessing, in short, during the past five years, both in international affairs and in industry, is the breakdown of the organization of society on the basis of rights divorced from obligations. Sooner or later the collapse was inevitable, because the basis was too narrow. For a right is simply a power which is secured by legal sanctions, " a capacity," as the lawyers define it, " residing in one man, of controlling, with the assistance of the State, the action of others," and a right should not be absolute for the same reason that a power should not be absolute. No doubt it is better that individuals should have absolute rights than that the State or the Government should have them; and it was the reaction against the abuses of absolute power by the State which led in the eighteenth century to the declaration of the absolute rights of individuals.

The most obvious defense against the assertion of one extreme was the assertion of the other. Because Governments and the relics of feudalism had encroached upon the property of individuals it was affirmed that the right of property was absolute; because they had strangled enterprise, it was affirmed that every man had a natural right to conduct his business as he pleased. But, in reality, both the one assertion and the other are false, and, if applied to practice, must lead to disaster. The State has no absolute rights; they are limited by its commission. The individual has no absolute rights; they are relative to the function which he performs in the community of which he is a member, because, unless they are so limited, the consequences must be something in the nature of private war. All rights, in short, are conditional and derivative, because all power should be conditional and derivative. They are derived from the end or purpose of the society in which they exist. They are conditional on being used to contribute to the attainment of that end, not to thwart it. And this means in practice that, if society is to be healthy, men must regard themselves not as the owners of rights, but as trustees for the discharge of functions and the instruments of a social purpose.

FIVE

PROPERTY AND CREATIVE WORK

♦

THE application of the principle that society should be organized upon the basis of functions, is not recondite, but simple and direct. It offers in the first place, a standard for discriminating between those types of private property which are legitimate and those which are not. During the last century and a half, political thought has oscillated between two conceptions of property, both of which, in their different ways, are extravagant. On the one hand, the practical foundation of social organization has been the doctrine that the particular forms of private property which exist at any moment are a thing sacred and inviolable, that anything may properly become the object of property rights, and that, when it does, the title to it is absolute and unconditioned. The modern industrial system took shape in an age when this theory of property was triumphant. The American Constitution and the French Declaration of the Rights of Man both treated property as one of the fundamental rights which Governments exist to protect. The English Revolution of 1688, undogmatic and reticent though it was, had in effect done the same. The great individualists from Locke to Turgot, Adam Smith and Bentham all repeated, in different language, a similar conception. Though what gave the Revolution its diabolical character in the eyes of the English upper classes was its treatment of property, the dogma of the sanctity of private property was maintained as tenaciously by French Jacobins as by English Tories; and the theory that property is an absolute, which is held by many modern Conservatives, is identical, if only they knew it, with that not only of the men of 1789, but of the Convention itself.

On the other hand, the attack has been almost as undiscriminating as the defense. "Private property" has been the central position against which the social movement of the last hundred years has directed its forces. The criticism of it has ranged from an imaginative communism in the most elementary and personal of necessaries, to prosaic and partially realized proposals to transfer certain kinds of property from private to public ownership, or to limit their exploitation by restrictions imposed by the State. But, however varying in emphasis and in method, the general note of what may conveniently be called the Socialist criticism of property is what the word Socialism itself implies. Its essence is the statement that the economic evils of society are primarily due to the unregulated operation, under modern conditions of industrial organization, of the institution of private property.

The divergence of opinion is natural, since in most discussions of property the opposing theorists have usually been discussing different things. Property is the most ambiguous of categories. It covers a multitude of rights which have nothing in common except that they are exercised by persons and enforced by the State.

Apart from these formal characteristics, they vary indefinitely in economic character, in social effect, and in moral justification. They may be conditional like the grant of patent rights, or absolute like the ownership of ground rents, terminable like copyright, or permanent like a freehold, as comprehensive as sovereignty or as restricted as an easement, as intimate and personal as the ownership of clothes and books, or as remote and intangible as shares in a gold mine or rubber plantation. It is idle, therefore, to present a case for or against private property without specifying the particular forms of property to which reference is made, and the journalist who says that " private property is the foundation of civilization " agrees with Proudhon, who said it was theft, in this respect at least that, without further definition, the words of both are meaningless. Arguments which support or demolish certain kinds of property may have no application to others; considerations which are conclusive in one stage of economic organization may be almost irrelevant in the next. The course of wisdom is neither to attack private property in general nor to defend it in general; for things are not similar in quality, merely because they are identical in name. It is to discriminate between the various concrete embodiments of what, in itself, is, after all, little more than an abstraction.

The origin and development of different kinds of proprietary rights is not material to this discussion. Whatever may have been the historical process by which they have been established and recognized, the *rationale* of private property traditional in England is that which sees in it the security that each man will reap where he has sown. "If I despair of enjoying the fruits of labor," said Bentham, repeating what were in all essentials the arguments of Locke, "I shall only live from day to day; I shall not undertake labors which will only benefit my enemies." Property, it is argued, is a moral right, and not merely a legal right, because it insures that the producer will not be deprived by violence of the result of his efforts. The period from which that doctrine was inherited differed from our own in three obvious, but significant, respects. Property in land and in the simple capital used in most industries was widely distributed. Before the rise of capitalist agriculture and capitalist industry, the ownership, or at any rate the secure and effective occupation, of land and tools by those who used them, was a condition precedent to effective work in the field or in the workshop. The forces which threatened property were the fiscal policy of Governments and in some countries, for example France, the decaying relics of feudalism. The interference both of the one and of the other involved the sacrifice of those who carried on useful labor to those who did not. To resist them was to protect not only property but industry, which was indissolubly connected with it. Too often, indeed, resistance was ineffective. Accustomed to the misery of the rural proprietor in France, Voltaire remarked with astonishment that in England the peasant may be rich, and "does not fear to increase the number of his beasts or to cover his roof with tiles." And the English Parliamentarians and the French philosophers who made the inviolability of property rights the center of their political theory, when they defended those who owned, were incidentally, if sometimes unintentionally, defending those who labored. They were protecting the yeoman or the master craftsman or the merchant from seeing the fruits of his toil squandered by the hangers-on at St. James or the courtly parasites of Versailles.

In such circumstances the doctrine which found the justification of private property in the fact that it enabled the industrious man to reap where he had sown, was not a paradox, but, as far as the mass of the population was concerned, almost a truism. Property was defended as the most sacred of rights. But it was defended as a right which was not only widely exercised, but which was indispensable to the performance of the active function of providing food and clothing. For it consisted predominantly of one of two types, land or tools which were used by the owner for the purpose of production, and personal possessions which were the necessities or amenities of civilized existence. The former had its *rationale* in the fact that the land of the peasant or the tools of the craftsman were the condition of his rendering the economic services which society required; the latter because furniture and clothes are indispensable to a life of decency and comfort. The proprietary rights—and, of course, they were numerous—which had their source, not in work, but in predatory force, were protected from criticism by the wide distribution of some kind of property among the mass of the population, and in England, at least, the cruder of them were gradually whittled down. When property in land and what simple capital existed were generally diffused among all classes of society, when, in most parts of England, the typical workman was not a laborer but a peasant or small master, who could point to the strips which he had plowed or the cloth which he had woven, when the greater part of the wealth passing at death consisted of land, household furniture and a stock in trade which was hardly distinguishable from it, the moral justification of the title to property was self-evident. It was obviously, what theorists said that it was, and plain men knew it to be, the labor spent in producing, acquiring and administering it.

Such property was not a burden upon society, but a condition of its health and efficiency, and indeed, of its continued existence. To protect it was to maintain the organization through which public necessities were supplied. If, as in Tudor England, the peasant was evicted from his holding to make room for sheep, or crushed, as in eighteenth century France, by arbitrary taxation and seignurial dues, land went out of cultivation and the whole community was short of food. If the tools of the carpenter or smith were seized, plows were not repaired or horses shod. Hence, before the rise of a commercial civilization, it was the mark of statesmanship, alike in the England of the Tudors and in the France of Henry IV, to cherish the small property-owner even to the point of offending the great. Popular sentiment idealized the yeoman—" the Joseph of the country who keeps the poor from starving "—not merely because he owned property, but because he worked on it, denounced that " bringing of the livings of many into the hands of one," which capitalist societies regard with equanimity as an inevitable, and, apparently, a laudable result of economic development, cursed the usurer who took advantage of his neighbor's necessities to live without labor, was shocked by the callous indifference to public welfare shown by those who " not having before their eyes either God or the profit and advantage of the realm, have enclosed with hedges and dykes towns and hamlets," and was sufficiently powerful to compel Governments to intervene to prevent the laying of field to field, and the engrossing of looms—to set limits, in short, to the scale to which property might grow.

When Bacon, who commended Henry VII for protecting the tenant right of the small farmer, and pleaded in the House of Commons for more drastic land legislation, wrote " Wealth is like muck. It is not good but if it be spread," he was expressing in an epigram what was the commonplace of every writer on politics from Fortescue at the end of the fifteenth century to Harrington in the middle of the seventeenth. The modern conservative, who is inclined to take *au pied de la lettre* the vigorous argument in which Lord Hugh Cecil denounces the doctrine that the maintenance of proprietary rights ought to be contingent upon the use to which they are put, may be reminded that Lord Hugh's own theory is of a kind to make his ancestors turn in their graves. Of the two members of the family who achieved distinction before the nineteenth century, the elder advised the Crown to prevent landlords evicting tenants, and actually proposed to fix a pecuniary maximum to the property which different classes might possess, while the younger attacked enclosing in Parliament, and carried legislation compelling landlords to build cottages, to let them with small holdings, and to plow up pasture.

William and Robert Cecil were sagacious and responsible men, and their view that the protection of property should be accompanied by the enforcement of obligations upon its owners was shared by most of their contemporaries. The idea that the institution of private property involves the right of the owner to use it, or refrain from using it, in such a way as he may please, and that its principal significance is to supply him with an income, irrespective of any duties which he may discharge, would not have been understood by most public men of that age, and, if understood, would have been repudiated with indignation by the more reputable among them. They found the meaning of property in the public purposes to which it contributed, whether they were the production of food, as among the peasantry, or the management of public affairs, as among the gentry, and hesitated neither to maintain those kinds of property which met these obligations nor to repress those uses of it which appeared likely to conflict with them. Property was to be an aid to creative work, not an alternative to it. The patentee was secured protection for a new invention, in order to secure him the fruits of his own brain, but the monopolist who grew fat on the industry of others was to be put down. The law of the village bound the peasant to use his land, not as he himself might find most profitable, but to grow the corn the village needed. Long after political changes had made direct interference impracticable, even the higher ranks of English landowners continued to dis-charge, however capriciously and tyrannically, duties which were vaguely felt to be the contribution which they made to the public service in virtue of their estates. When as in France, the obligations of ownership were repudiated almost as completely as they have been by the owner of to-day, nemesis came in an onslaught upon the position of a *noblesse* which had retained its rights and abdicated its functions. Property reposed, in short, not merely upon convenience, or the appetite for gain, but on a moral principle. It was protected not only for the sake of those who owned, but for the sake of those who worked and of those for whom their work provided. It was protected, because, without security for property, wealth could not be produced or the business of society carried on.

Whatever the future may contain, the past has shown no more excellent social order than that in which the mass of the people were the masters of the holdings which they plowed and of the tools with which they worked, and could boast, with the English freeholder, that " it is a quietness to a man's mind to live upon his own and to know his heir certain." With this con-ception of property and its practical expression in social institutions those who urge that society should be organized on the basis of function have no quarrel. It is in agreement with their own doctrine, since it justifies property by reference to the services which it enables its owner to perform. All that they need ask is that it should be carried to its logical conclusion.

For the argument has evidently more than one edge. If it justifies certain types of property, it condemns others; and in the conditions of modern industrial civilization, what it justifies is less than what it condemns. The truth is, indeed, that this theory of property and the institutions in which it is embodied have survived into an age in which the whole structure of society is radically different from that in which it was formulated, and which made it a valid argument, if not for all, at least for the most common and characteristic kinds of property. It is not merely that the ownership of any substantial share in the national wealth is concentrated to-day in the hands of a few hundred thousand families, and that at the end of an age which began with an affirmation of the rights of property, proprietary rights are, in fact, far from being widely distributed. Nor is it merely that what makes property insecure to-day is not the arbitrary taxation of unconstitutional monarchies or the privileges of an idle *noblesse,* but the insatiable expansion and aggregation of property itself, which menaces with absorption all property less than the greatest, the small master, the little shopkeeper, the country bank, and has turned the mass of mankind into a proletariat working under the agents and for the profit of those who own.

The characteristic fact, which differentiates most

modern property from that of the pre-industrial age, and which turns against it the very reasoning by which formerly it was supported, is that in modern economic conditions ownership is not active, but passive, that to most of those who own property to-day it is not a means of work but an instrument for the acquisition of gain or the exercise of power, and that there is no guarantee that gain bears any relation to service, or power to responsibility. For property which can be regarded as a condition of the performance of function, like the tools of the craftsman, or the holding of the peasant, or the personal possessions which contribute to a life of health and efficiency, forms an insignificant proportion, as far as its value is concerned, of the property rights existing at present. In modern industrial societies the great mass of property consists, as the annual review of wealth passing at death reveals, neither of personal acquisitions such as household furniture, nor of the owner's stock-in-trade, but of rights of various kinds, such as royalties, ground-rents, and, above all, of course shares in industrial undertakings which yield an income irrespective of any personal service rendered by their owners. Ownership and use are normally divorced. The greater part of modern property has been attenuated to a pecuniary lien or bond on the product of industry which carries with it a right to payment, but which is normally valued precisely because it relieves the owner from any obligation to perform a positive or constructive function.

Such property may be called passive property, or property for acquisition, for exploitation, or for power, to distinguish it from the property which is actively used by its owner for the conduct of his profession or the upkeep of his household. To the lawyer the first is, of course, as fully property as the second. It is questionable, however, whether economists shall call it " Property " at all, and not rather, as Mr. Hobson has suggested, " Improperty," since it is not identical with the rights which secure the owner the produce of his toil, but is opposite of them. A classification of proprietary rights based upon this difference would be instructive. If they were arranged according to the closeness with which they approximate to one or other of these two extremes, it would be found that they were spread along a line stretching from property which is obviously the payment for, and condition of, personal services, to property which is merely a right to payment from the services rendered by others, in fact a private tax. The rough order which would emerge, if all details and qualification were omitted, might be something as follows:—

1. Property in payments made for personal services.

2. Property in personal possessions necessary to health and comfort.

3. Property in land and tools used by their owners.

4. Property in copyright and patent rights owned by authors and inventors.

5. Property in pure interest, including much agricultural rent.

6. Property in profits of luck and good fortune: " quasi-rents."

7. Property in monopoly profits.

8. Property in urban ground rents.

9. Property in royalties.

The first four kinds of property obviously accompany, and in some sense condition, the performance of work. The last four obviously do not. Pure interest has some affinities with both. It represents a necessary economic cost, the equivalent of which must be born, whatever the legal arrangements under which property is held, and is thus unlike the property representd by profits (other than the equivalent of salaries and payment for necessary risk), urban ground-rents and royalties. It relieves the recipient from personal services, and thus resembles them.

The crucial question for any society is, under which each of these two broad groups of categories the greater part (measured in value) of the proprietary rights which it maintains are at any given moment to be found. If they fall in the first group creative work will be encouraged and idleness will be depressed; if they fall in the second, the result will be the reverse. The facts vary widely from age to age and from country to country. Nor have they ever been fully revealed; for the lords of the jungle do not hunt by daylight. It is probable, at least, that in the England of 1550 to 1750, a larger proportion of the existing property consisted of land and tools used by their owners than either in contemporary France, where feudal dues absorbed a considerable proportion of the peasants' income, or than in the England of 1800 to 1850, where the new capitalist manufacturers made hundreds per cent. while manual workers were goaded by starvation into ineffectual revolt. It is probable that in the nineteenth century, thanks to the Revolution, France and England changed places, and that in this respect not only Ireland but the British Dominions resemble the former rather than the latter. The transformation can be studied best of all in the United States, in parts of which the population of peasant proprietors and small masters of the early nineteenth century were replaced in three generations by a propertyless proletariat and a capitalist plutocracy. The abolition of the economic privileges of agrarian feudalism, which, under the name of equality, was the driving force of the French Revolution, and which has taken place, in one form or another, in all countries touched by its influence, has been largely counterbalanced since 1800 by the growth of the inequalities springing from Industrialism.

In England the general effect of recent economic development has been to swell proprietary rights which entitle the owners to payment without work, and to diminish those which can properly be described as functional. The expansion of the former, and the process by which the simpler forms of property have been merged in them, are movements the significance of which it is hardly possible to over-estimate. There is, of course, a considerable body of property which is still of the older type. But though working landlords, and capitalists who manage their own businesses, are still in the aggregate a numerous body, the organization for which they stand is not that which is most representative of the modern economic world. The general tendency for the ownership and administration of prop-

erty to be separated, the general refinement of property
into a claim on goods produced by an unknown worker,
is as unmistakable as the growth of capitalist industry
and urban civilization themselves. Villages are turned
into towns and property in land changes from the holding worked by a farmer or the estate administered by a
landlord into " rents," which are advertised and bought
and sold like any other investment. Mines are opened
and the rights of the landowner are converted into a
tribute for every ton of coal which is brought to the
surface. As joint-stock companies take the place of the
individual enterprise which was typical of the earlier
years of the factory system, organization passes from the
employer who both owns and manages his business, into
the hands of salaried officials, and again the mass of
property-owners is swollen by the multiplication of
rentiers who put their wealth at the disposal of industry, but who have no other connection with it. The
change is taking place in our day most conspicuously,
perhaps, through the displacement in retail trade of the
small shopkeeper by the multiple store, and the substitution in manufacturing industry of combines and amal-
gamations for separate businesses conducted by competing employers. And, of course, it is not only by economic development that such claims are created. " Out
of the eater came forth meat, and out of the strong
came forth sweetness." It is probable that war, which in
barbarous ages used to be blamed as destructive of
property, has recently created more titles to property
than almost all other causes put together.

Infinitely diverse as are these proprietary rights, they

have the common characteristic of being so entirely separated from the actual objects over which they are exercised, so rarified and generalized, as to be analogous almost to a form of currency rather than to the property which is so closely united to its owner as to seem a part of him. Their isolation from the rough environment of economic life, where the material objects of which they are the symbol are shaped and handled, is their charm. It is also their danger. The hold which a class has upon the future depends on the function which it performs. What nature demands is work: few working aristocracies, however tyrannical, have fallen; few functionless aristocracies have survived. In society, as in the world of organic life, atrophy is but one stage removed from death. In proportion as the landowner becomes a mere *rentier* and industry is conducted, not by the rude energy of the competing employers who dominated its infancy, but by the salaried servants of shareholders, the argument for private property which reposes on the impossibility of finding any organization to supersede them loses its application, for they are already superseded.

Whatever may be the justification of these types of property, it cannot be that which was given for the property of the peasant or the craftsman. It cannot be that they are necessary in order to secure to each man the fruits of his own labor. For if a legal right which gives £50,000 a year to a mineral owner in the North of England and to a ground landlord in London " secures the fruits of labor " at all, the fruits are the proprietor's and the labor that of some one else. Property has no more insidious enemies than those well-meaning anarchists who, by defending all forms of it as equally valid, involve the institution in the discredit attaching to its extravagances.   In reality, whatever conclusion may be drawn from the fact, the greater part of modern property, whether, like mineral rights and urban ground-rents, it is merely a form of private taxation which the law allows certain persons to levy on the industry of others, or whether, like property in capital, it consists of rights to payment for instruments which the capitalist cannot himself use but puts at the disposal of those who can, has as its essential feature that it confers upon its owners income unaccompanied by personal service.   In this respect the ownership of land and the ownership of capital are normally similar, though from other points of view their differences are important.   To the economist rent and interest are distinguished by the fact that the latter, though it is often accompanied by surplus elements which are merged with it in dividends, is the price of an instrument of production which would not be forthcoming for industry if the price were not paid, while the former is a differential surplus which does not affect the supply.   To the business community and the solicitor land and capital are equally investments, between which, since they possess the common characteristic of yielding income without labor, it is inequitable to discriminate; and though their significance as economic categories may be different, their effect as social institutions is the same.   It is to separate property from creative ability, and to divide society into two classes, of which one has its primary interest in passive ownership, while the other is mainly dependent upon active work.

Hence the real analogy to many kinds of modern property is not the simple property of the small land-owner or the craftsman, still less the household goods and dear domestic amenities, which is what the word suggests to the guileless minds of clerks and shopkeepers, and which stampede them into displaying the ferocity of terrified sheep when the cry is raised that " Property " is threatened. It is the feudal dues which robbed the French peasant of part of his produce till the Revolution abolished them. How do royalties differ from *quintaines* and *lods et ventes?* They are similar in their origin and similar in being a tax levied on each increment of wealth which labor produces. How do urban ground-rents differ from the payments which were made to English sinecurists before the Reform Bill of 1832 ? They are equally tribute paid by those who work to those who do not. If the monopoly profits of the owner of *banalités,* whose tenant must grind corn at his mill and make wine at his press, were an intolerable oppression, what is the sanctity attaching to the monopoly profits of the capitalists, who, as the Report of the Government Committee on trusts tells us, " in soap, tobacco, wall-paper, salt, cement and in the textile trades . . . are in a position to control output and prices " or, in other words, can compel the consumer to buy from them, at the figure they fix, on pain of not buying at all ?

All these rights—royalties, ground-rents, monopoly profits—are " Property." The criticism most fatal to them is not that of Socialists. It is contained in the

arguments by which property is usually defended. For
if the meaning of the institution is to encourage industry by securing that the worker shall receive the produce
of his toil, then precisely in proportion as it is important
to preserve the property which a man has in the results
of his own efforts, is it important to abolish that which
he has in the results of the efforts of some one else. The
considerations which justify ownership as a function are
those which condemn it as a tax. Property is not theft,
but a good deal of theft becomes property. The owner
of royalties who, when asked why he should be paid
£50,000 a year from minerals which he has neither
discovered nor developed nor worked but only owned,
replies " But it's Property ! " may feel all the awe
which his language suggests. But in reality he is be-
having like the snake which sinks into its background
by pretending that it is the dead branch of a tree, or
the lunatic who tried to catch rabbits by sitting behind
a hedge and making a noise like a turnip. He is prac-
tising protective—and sometimes aggressive—mimicry.
His sentiments about property are those of the simple
toiler who fears that what he has sown another may
reap. His claim is to be allowed to continue to reap
what another has sown.

It is sometimes suggested that the less attractive characteristics of our industrial civilization, its combination
of luxury and squalor, its class divisions and class
warfare, are accidental maladjustments which are not
rooted in the center of its being, but are excrescences
which economic progress itself may in time be expected
to correct. That agreeable optimism will not survive an

examination of the operation of the institution of private property in land and capital in industrialized communities. In countries where land is widely distributed,
in France or in Ireland, its effect may be to produce
a general diffusion of wealth among a rural middle
class who at once work and own. In countries where
the development of industrial organization has separated the ownership of property and the performance of
work, the normal effect of private property is to transfer to functionless owners the surplus arising from the
more fertile sites, the better machinery, the more elaborate organization. No clearer exemplifications of this
" law of rent " has been given than the figures supplied
to the Coal Industry Commission by Sir Arthur Lowes
Dickenson, which showed that in a given quarter the
costs per ton of producing coal varied from 12s. 6d. to
48s. 0d. per ton, and the profits from *nil* to 16s. 6d. The
distribution in dividends to shareholders of the surplus
accruing from the working of richer and more acces-
sible seams, from special opportunities and access to
markets, from superior machinery, management and organization, involves the establishment of Privilege as a
national institution, as much as the most arbitrary exac-
tions of a feudal *seigneur*. It is the foundation of an
inequality which is not accidental or temporary, but
necessary and permanent. And on this inequality is
erected the whole apparatus of class institutions, which
make not only the income, but the housing, education,
health and manners, indeed the very physical appearance of different classes of Englishmen almost as different from each other as though the minority were

alien settlers established amid the rude civilization of a race of impoverished aborigines.

So the justification of private property traditional in England, which saw in it the security that each man would enjoy the fruits of his own labor, though largely applicable to the age in which it was formulated, has undergone the fate of most political theories. It has been refuted not by the doctrines of rival philosophers, but by the prosaic course of economic development. As far as the mass of mankind are concerned, the need which private property other than personal possessions does still often satisfy, though imperfectly and precariously, is the need for security. To the small investors, who are the majority of property-owners, though owning only an insignificant fraction of the property in existence, its meaning is simple. It is not wealth or power, or even leisure from work. It is safety. They work hard. They save a little money for old age, or for sickness, or for their children. They invest it, and the interest stands between them and all that they dread most. Their savings are of convenience to industry, the income from them is convenient to themselves. "Why," they ask, "should we not reap in old age the advantage of energy and thrift in youth?" And this hunger for security is so imperious that those who suffer most from the abuses of property, as well as those who, if they could profit by them, would be least inclined to do so, will tolerate and even defend them, for fear lest the knife which trims dead matter should cut into the quick. They have seen too many men drown to be critical of dry land, though it be an inhospitable rock. They are haunted by the nightmare of the future, and, if a burglar broke it, would welcome a burglar.

This need for security is fundamental, and almost the gravest indictment of our civilization is that the mass of mankind are without it. Property is one way of organizing it. It is quite comprehensible therefore, that the instrument should be confused with the end, and that any proposal to modify it should create dismay. In the past, human beings, roads, bridges and ferries, civil, judicial and clerical offices, and commissions in the army have all been private property. Whenever it was proposed to abolish the rights exercised over them, it was protested that their removal would involve the destruction of an institution in which thrifty men had invested their savings, and on which they depended for protection amid the chances of life and for comfort in old age. In fact, however, property is not the only method of assuring the future, nor, when it is the way selected, is security dependent upon the maintenance of all the rights which are at present normally involved in ownership. In so far as its psychological foundation is the necessity for securing an income which is stable and certain, which is forthcoming when its recipient cannot work, and which can be used to provide for those who cannot provide for themselves, what is really demanded is not the command over the fluctuating proceeds of some particular undertaking, which accompanies the ownership of capital, but the security which is offered by an annuity. Property is the instrument, security is the object, and when some alternative way is forthcoming of providing the latter, it does not appear in practice that any loss of confidence. or freedom or independence is caused by the absence of the former.

Hence not only the manual workers, who since the rise of capitalism, have rarely in England been able to accumulate property sufficient to act as a guarantee of income when their period of active earning is past, but also the middle and professional classes, increasingly seek security to-day, not in investment, but in insurance against sickness and death, in the purchase of annuities, or in what is in effect the same thing, the accumulation of part of their salary towards a pension which is paid when their salary ceases. The professional man may buy shares in the hope of making a profit on the transaction. But when what he desires to buy is security, the form which his investment takes is usually one kind or another of insurance. The teacher, or nurse, or government servant looks forward to a pension. Women, who fifty years ago would have been regarded as dependent almost as completely as if femininity were an incurable disease with which they had been born, and whose fathers, unless rich men, would have been tormented with anxiety for fear lest they should not save sufficient to provide for them, now receive an education, support themselves in professions, and save in the same way. It is still only in comparatively few cases that this type of provision is made; almost all wage-earners outside government employment, and many in it, as well as large numbers of professional men, have nothing to fall back upon in sickness or old age. But that does not alter the fact that, when it is made, it meets the need for security, which, apart, of course, from personal possessions and household furniture, is the principal meaning of property to by far the largest element in the population, and that it meets it more completely and certainly than property itself.

Nor, indeed, even when property is the instrument used to provide for the future, is such provision dependent upon the maintenance in its entirety of the whole body of rights which accompany ownership to-day. Property is not simple but complex. That of a man who has invested his savings as an ordinary shareholder comprises at least three rights, the right to interest, the right to profits, the right to control. In so far as what is desired is the guarantee for the maintenance of a stable income, not the acquisition of additional wealth without labor—in so far as his motive is not gain but security—the need is met by interest on capital. It has no necessary connection either with the right to residuary profits or the right to control the management of the undertaking from which the profits are derived, both of which are vested to-day in the shareholder. If all that were desired were to use property as an instrument for purchasing security, the obvious course—from the point of view of the investor desiring to insure his future the safest course—would be to assimilate his position as far as possible to that of a debenture holder or mortgagee, who obtains the stable income which is his motive for investment, but who neither incurs the risks nor receives the profits of the speculator. To insist that the elaborate apparatus of proprietary rights which dis-

tributes dividends of thirty per cent to the shareholders
in Coats, and several thousands a year to the owner of
mineral royalties and ground-rents, and then allows
them to transmit the bulk of gains which they have not
earned to descendants who in their turn will thus be
relieved from the necessity of earning, must be maintained for the sake of the widow and the orphan, the
vast majority of whom have neither and would gladly
part with them all for a safe annuity if they had, is,
to say the least of it, extravagantly *mal-à-propos*. It is
like pitching a man into the water because he expresses
a wish for a bath, or presenting a tiger cub to a house-
holder who is plagued with mice, on the ground that
tigers and cats both belong to the genus *felis*. The tiger
hunts for itself not for its masters, and when game is
scarce will hunt them. The classes who own little or no
property may reverence it because it is security. But
the classes who own much prize it for quite different
reasons, and laugh in their sleeve at the innocence which
supposes that anything as vulgar as the savings of the
petite bourgeoisie have, except at elections, any interest
for them. They prize it because it is the order which
quarters them on the community and which provides for
the maintenance of a leisure class at the public expense.

" Possession," said the Egoist, " without obligation to
the object possessed, approaches felicity." Functionless
property appears natural to those who believe that society should be organized for the acquisition of private
wealth, and attacks upon it perverse or malicious, because the question which they ask of any institution is,
" What does it yield ? "   And such property yields much

to those who own it. Those, however, who hold that social unity and effective work are possible only if society is organized and wealth distributed on the basis of function, will ask of an institution, not, "What dividends does it pay?" but "What service does it perform?" To them the fact that much property yields income irrespective of any service which is performed or obligation which is recognized by its owners will appear not a quality but a vice. They will see in the social confusion which it produces, payments disproportionate to service here, and payments without any service at all there, and dissatisfaction everywhere, a convincing confirmation of their argument that to build on a foundation of rights and of rights alone is to build on a quicksand.

From the portentous exaggeration into an absolute of what once was, and still might be, a sane and social institution most other social evils follow the power of those who do not work over those who do, the alternate subservience and rebelliousness of those who work towards those who do not, the starving of science and thought and creative effort for fear that expenditure upon them should impinge on the comfort of the sluggard and the *fainéant,* and the arrangement of society in most of its subsidiary activities to suit the convenience not of those who work usefully but of those who spend gaily, so that the most hideous, desolate and parsimonious places in the country are those in which the greatest wealth is produced, the Clyde valley, or the cotton towns of Lancashire, or the mining villages of Scotland and Wales, and the gayest and most luxurious those in which it is consumed. From the point of view of social health and economic efficiency, society should obtain its material equipment at the cheapest price possible, and after providing for depreciation and expansion should distribute the whole product to its working members and their dependents. What happens at present, however, is that its workers are hired at the cheapest price which the market (as modified by organization) allows, and that the surplus, somewhat diminished by taxation, is distributed to the owners of property. Profits may vary in a given year from a loss to 100 per cent. But wages are fixed at a level which will enable the marginal firm to continue producing one year with another; and the surplus, even when due partly to efficient management, goes neither to managers nor manual workers, but to shareholders. The meaning of the process becomes startlingly apparent when, as in Lancashire to-day, large blocks of capital change hands at a period of abnormal activity. The existing shareholders receive the equivalent of the capitalized expectation of future profits. The workers, as workers, do not participate in the immense increment in value; and when, in the future, they demand an advance in wages, they will be met by the answer that profits, which before the transaction would have been reckoned large, yield shareholders after it only a low rate of interest on their investment.

The truth is that whereas in earlier ages the protection of property was normally the protection of work, the relationship between them has come in the course of the economic development of the last two centuries to be very nearly reversed. The two elements which compose civilization are active effort and passive property, the labor of human things and the tools which human beings use. Of these two elements those who supply the first maintain and improve it, those who own the second normally dictate its character, its development and its administration. Hence, though politically free, the mass of mankind live in effect under rules imposed to protect the interests of the small section among them whose primary concern is ownership. From this subordination of creative activity to passive property, the worker who depends upon his brains, the organizer, inventor, teacher or doctor suffers almost as much embarrassment as the craftsman. The real economic cleavage is not, as is often said, between employers and employed, but between all who do constructive work, from scientist to laborer, on the one hand, and all whose main interest is the preservation of existing proprietary rights upon the other, irrespective of whether they contribute to constructive work or not.

If, therefore, under the modern conditions which have concentrated any substantial share of property in the hands of a small minority of the population, the world is to be governed for the advantages of those who own, it is only incidentally and by accident that the results will be agreeable to those who work. In practice there is a constant collision between them. Turned into another channel, half the wealth distributed in dividends to functionless shareholders, could secure every child a good education up to 18, could re-endow English Universities, and (since more efficient production is important) could equip English industries for more efficient production. Half the ingenuity now applied to the protection of property could have made most industrial diseases as rare as smallpox, and most English cities into places of health and even of beauty. What stands in the way is the doctrine that the rights of property are absolute, irrespective of any social function which its owners may perform. So the laws which are most stringently enforced are still the laws which protect property, though the protection of property is no longer likely to be equivalent to the protection of work, and the interests which govern industry and predominate in public affairs are proprietary interests. A mill-owner may poison or mangle a generation of operatives; but his brother magistrates will let him off with a caution or a nominal fine to poison and mangle the next. For he is an owner of property. A landowner may draw rents from slums in which young children die at the rate of 200 per 1000; but he will be none the less welcome in polite society. For property has no obligations and therefore can do no wrong. Urban land may be held from the market on the outskirts of cities in which human beings are living three to a room, and rural land may be used for sport when villagers are leaving it to overcrowd them still more. No public authority intervenes, for both are property. To those who believe that institutions which repudiate all moral significance must sooner or later collapse, a society which confuses the protection of property with the preservation of its functionless perversions will appear as precarious as that which has left the memorials of its tasteless frivolity and more tasteless ostentation in the gardens of Versailles.

Do men love peace? They will see the greatest enemy of social unity in rights which involve no obligation to co-operate for the service of society. Do they value equality? Property rights which dispense their owners from the common human necessity of labor make inequality an institution permeating every corner of society, from the distribution of material wealth to the training of intellect itself. Do they desire greater industrial efficiency? There is no more fatal obstacle to efficiency than the revelation that idleness has the same privileges as industry, and that for every additional blow with the pick or hammer an additional profit will be distributed among shareholders who wield neither.

Indeed, functionless property is the greatest enemy of legitimate property itself. It is the parasite which kills the organism that produced it. Bad money drives out good, and, as the history of the last two hundred years shows, when property for acquisition or power and property for service or for use jostle each other freely in the market, without restrictions such as some legal systems have imposed on alienation and inheritance, the latter tends normally to be absorbed by the former, because it has less resisting power. Thus functionless property grows, and as it grows it undermines the creative energy which produced property and which in earlier ages it protected. It cannot unite men, for what unites them is the bond of service to a common purpose, and that bond it repudiates, since its very essence is the maintenance of rights irrespective of service. It cannot create; it can only spend, so that the number of scientists, inventors, artists or men of letters who have sprung in the course of the last century from hereditary riches can be numbered on one hand. It values neither culture nor beauty, but only the power which belongs to wealth and the ostentation which is the symbol of it.

So those who dread these qualities, energy and thought and the creative spirit—and they are many—will not discriminate, as we have tried to discriminate, between different types and kinds of property, in order that they may preserve those which are legitimate and abolish those which are not. They will endeavor to preserve all private property, even in its most degenerate forms. And those who value those things will try to promote them by relieving property of its perversions, and thus enabling it to return to its true nature. They will not desire to establish any visionary communism, for they will realize that the free disposal of a sufficiency of personal possessions is the condition of a healthy and self-respecting life, and will seek to distribute more widely the property rights which make them to-day the privilege of a minority. But they will refuse to submit to the naïve philosophy which would treat all proprietary rights as equal in sanctity merely because they are identical in name. They will distinguish sharply between property which is used by its owner for the conduct of his profession or the upkeep of his household, and property which is merely a claim on wealth produced by another's labor. They will insist that property is moral and healthy only when it is used as a condition not of idleness but of activity, and when it involves the discharge of definite personal obligations. They will endeavor, in short, to base it upon the principle of function.

SIX

THE FUNCTIONAL SOCIETY

♦

THE application to property and industry of the principle of function is compatible with several different types of social organization, and is as unlikely as more important revelations to be the secret of those who cry " Lo here ! " and " Lo there ! " The essential thing is that men should fix their minds upon the idea of purpose, and give that idea pre-eminence over all subsidiary issues. If, as is patent, the purpose of industry is to provide the material foundation of a good social life, then any measure which makes that provision more effective, so long as it does not conflict with some still more important purpose, is wise, and any institution which thwarts or encumbers it is foolish. It is foolish, for example, to cripple education, as it is crippled in England for the sake of industry; for one of the uses of industry is to provide the wealth which may make possible better education. It is foolish to maintain property rights for which no service is performed, for payment without service is waste; and if it is true, as statisticians affirm, that, even were income equally divided, income per head would be small, then it is all the more foolish, for sailors in a boat have no room for first-class passengers, and it is all the more important that none of the small national income should be misapplied. It is foolish to leave the direction of industry in the hands of servants of private property-owners who themselves know nothing about it but its balance sheets, because this is to divert it from the performance of service to the acquisition of gain, and to subordinate those who do creative work to those who do not.

The course of wisdom in the affairs of industry is, after all, what it is in any other department of organized life. It is to consider the end for which economic activity is carried on and then to adapt economic organization to it. It is to pay for service and for service only, and when capital is hired to make sure that it is hired at the cheapest possible price. It is to place the responsibility for organizing industry on the shoulders of those who work and use, not of those who own, because production is the business of the producer and the proper person to see that he discharges his business is the consumer for whom, and not for the owner of property, it ought to be carried on. Above all it is to insist that all industries shall be conducted in complete publicity as to costs and profits, because publicity ought to be the antiseptic both of economic and political abuses, and no man can have confidence in his neighbor unless both work in the light.

As far as property is concerned, such a policy would possess two edges. On the one hand, it would aim at abolishing those forms of property in which ownership is divorced from obligations. On the other hand, it would seek to encourage those forms of economic organization under which the worker, whether owner or not, is free to carry on his work without sharing its control or its profits with the mere *rentier*. Thus, if in certain spheres it involved an extension of public ownership, it would in others foster an extension of private property. For it is not private ownership, but private ownership divorced from work, which is corrupting to the principle of industry; and the idea of some socialists that private property in land or capital is necessarily mischievous is a piece of scholastic pedantry as absurd as that of those conservatives who would invest all property with some kind of mysterious sanctity. It all depends what sort of property it is and for what purpose it is used. Provided that the State retains its eminent domain, and controls alienation, as it does under the Homestead laws of the Dominions, with sufficient stringency to prevent the creation of a class of functionless property-owners, there is no inconsistency between encouraging simultaneously a multiplication of peasant farmers and small masters who own their own farms or shops, and the abolition of private ownership in those industries, unfortunately to-day the most conspicuous, in which the private owner is an absentee shareholder.

Indeed, the second reform would help the first. In so far as the community tolerates functionless property it makes difficult, if not impossible, the restoration of the small master in agriculture or in industry, who cannot easily hold his own in a world dominated by great estates or capitalist finance. In so far as it abolishes those kinds of property which are merely parasitic, it facilitates the restoration of the small property-owner in those kinds of industry for which small ownership is adapted. A socialistic policy towards the former is not antagonistic to the " distributive state," but, in modern economic conditions, a necessary preliminary to it, and if by " Property " is meant the personal possessions which the word suggests to nine-tenths of the population, the object of socialists is not to undermine property but to protect and increase it. The boundary between large scale and small scale production will always be uncertain and fluctuating, depending, as it does, on technical conditions which cannot be foreseen: a cheapening of electrical power, for example, might result in the decentralization of manufactures, as steam resulted in their concentration. The fundamental issue, however, is not between different scales of ownership, but between ownership of different kinds, not between the large farmer or master and the small, but between property which is used for work and property which yields income without it. The Irish landlord was abolished, not because he owned a large scale, but because he was an owner and nothing more; if, and when English landownership has been equally attenuated, as in towns it already has been, it will deserve to meet the same fate. Once the issue of the character of ownership has been settled, the question of the size of the economic unit can be left to settle itself.

The first step, then, towards the organization of economic life for the performance of function is to abolish those types of private property in return for which no function is performed. The man who lives by owning without working is necessarily supported by the industry of some one else, and is, therefore, too expensive a luxury to be encouraged. Though he deserves to be treated with the leniency which ought to be, and usually is not, shown to those who have been brought up from infancy to any other disreputable trade, indulgence to individuals must not condone the institution of which both they and their neighbors are the victims. Judged by this standard, certain kinds of property are obviously anti-social. The rights in virtue of which the owner of the surface is entitled to levy a tax, called a royalty, on every ton of coal which the miner brings to the surface, to levy another tax, called a way-leave, on every ton of coal transported under the surface of his land though its amenity and value may be quite unaffected, to distort, if he pleases, the development of a whole district by refusing access to the minerals except upon his own terms, and to cause some 3,500 to 4,000 million tons to be wasted in barriers between different properties, while he in the meantime contributes to a chorus of lamentation over the wickedness of the miners in not producing more tons of coal for the public and incidentally more private taxes for himself—all this adds an agreeable touch of humor to the drab quality of our industrial civilization for which mineral owners deserve perhaps some recognition, though not the £100,000 odd a year which is paid to each of the four leading players, or the £6,000,000 a year which is distributed among the crowd.

The alchemy by which a gentleman who has never seen a coal mine distills the contents of that place of gloom into elegant chambers in London and a place in the country is not the monopoly of royalty owners. A similar feat of presdigitation is performed by the owner of urban ground-rents. In rural districts some landlords, perhaps many landlords, are partners in the hazardous and difficult business of agriculture, and, though they may often exercise a power which is socially excessive, the position which they hold and the income which they receive are, in part at last, a return for the functions which they perform. The ownership of urban land has been refined till of that crude ore only the pure gold is left. It is the perfect sinecure, for the only function it involves is that of collecting its profits, and in an age when the struggle of Liberalism against sinecures was still sufficiently recent to stir some chords of memory, the last and greatest of liberal thinkers drew the obvious deduction. " The reasons which form the justification . . . of property in land," wrote Mill in 1848, " are valid only in so far as the proprietor of land is its improver. . . . In no sound theory of private property was it ever contemplated that the proprietor of land should be merely a sinecurist quartered on it." Urban ground-rents and royalties are, in fact, as the Prime Minister in his unregenerate days suggested, a tax which some persons are permitted by the law to levy upon the industry of others. They differ from public taxation only in that their amount increases in proportion not to the nation's need of revenue but to its need of the coal and space on which they are levied, that their growth inures to private gain not to public benefit, and that if the proceeds are wasted on frivolous expenditure no one has any right to complain, because the arrangement by which Lord Smith spends wealth produced by Mr. Brown on objects which do no good to either is part of the system which, under the name of private property, Mr. Brown as well as Lord Smith have learned to regard as essential to the higher welfare of mankind.

But if we accept the principle of function we shall ask what is the *purpose* of this arrangement, and for what *end* the inhabitants of, for example, London pay £16,000,000 a year to their ground landlords. And if we find that it is for no purpose and no end, but that these things are like the horseshoes and nails which the City of London presents to the Crown on account of land in the Parish of St. Clement Danes, then we shall not deal harshly with a quaint historical survival, but neither shall we allow it to distract us from the business of the present, as though there had been history but there were not history any longer. We shall close these channels through which wealth leaks away by resuming the ownership of minerals and of urban land, as some communities in the British Dominions and on the Continent of Europe have resumed it already. We shall secure that such large accumulations as remain change hands at least once in every generation, by increasing our taxes on inheritance till what passes to the heir is little more than personal possessions, not the right to a tribute from industry which, though qualified by death-duties, is what the son of a rich man inherits to-day. We shall treat mineral owners and landowners, in short, as Plato would have treated the poets, whom in their ability to make something out of nothing and to bewitch mankind with words they a little resemble, and crown them with flowers and usher them politely out of the State.

SEVEN

INDUSTRY AS A PROFESSION

◆

Rights without functions are like the shades in Homer which drank blood but scattered trembling at the voice of a man. To extinguish royalties and urban ground-rents is merely to explode a superstition. It needs as little—and as much—resolution as to put one's hand through any other ghost. In all industries except the diminishing number in which the capitalist is himself the manager, property in capital is almost equally passive. Almost, but not quite. For, though the majority of its owners do not themselves exercise any positive function, they appoint those who do. It is true, of course, that the question of how capital is to be owned is distinct from the question of how it is to be administered, and that the former can be settled without prejudice to the latter. To infer, because shareholders own capital which is indispensable to industry, that therefore industry is dependent upon the maintenance of capital in the hands of shareholders, to write, with some economists, as though, if private property in capital were further attenuated or abolished altogether, the constructive energy of the managers who may own capital or may not, but rarely, in the more important industries, own more than a small fraction of it, must necessarily be impaired, is to be guilty of a robust *non-sequitur* and to ignore the most obvious facts of contemporary industry. The less the mere capitalist talks about the necessity for the consumer of an efficient organization of industry, the better; for, whatever the future of industry may be, an efficient organization is likely to have no room for *him*. But though shareholders do not govern, they reign, at least to the extent of saying once a year " *le roy le veult.*" If their rights are pared down or extinguished, the necessity for some organ to exercise them will still remain. And the question of the ownership of capital has this much in common with the question of industrial organization, that the problem of the constitution under which industry is to be conducted is common to both.

That constitution must be sought by considering how industry can be organized to express most perfectly the principle of purpose. The application to industry of the principle of purpose is simple, however difficult it may be to give effect to it. It is to turn it into a Profession. A Profession may be defined most simply as a trade which is organized, incompletely, no doubt, but genuinely, for the performance of function. It is not simply a collection of individuals who get a living for themselves by the same kind of work. Nor is it merely a group which is organized exclusively for the economic protection of its members, though that is normally among its purposes. It is a body of men who carry on their work in accordance with rules designed to enforce certain standards both for the better protection of its members and for the better service of the public. The standards which it maintains may be high or low: all professions have some rules which protect the interests

of the community and others which are an imposition on
it. Its essence is that it assumes certain responsibilities
for the competence of its members or the quality of its
wares, and that it deliberately prohibits certain kinds
of conduct on the ground that, though they may be
profitable to the individual, they are calculated to bring
into disrepute the organization to which he belongs.
While some of its rules are trade union regulations designed primarily to prevent the economic standards of
the profession being lowered by unscrupulous competition, others have as their main object to secure that no
member of the profession shall have any but a purely
professional interest in his work, by excluding the incentive of speculative profit.

The conception implied in the words " unprofessional
conduct " is, therefore, the exact opposite of the theory
and practice which assume that the service of the public
is best secured by the unrestricted pursuit on the part
of rival traders of their pecuniary self-interest, within
such limits as the law allows. It is significant that at
the time when the professional classes had deified free
competition as the arbiter of commerce and industry,
they did not dream of applying it to the occupations in
which they themselves were primarily interested, but
maintained, and indeed, elaborated machinery through
which a professional conscience might find expression.
The rules themselves may sometimes appear to the lay-
man arbitrary and ill-conceived. But their object is
clear. It is to impose on the profession itself the obligation of maintaining the quality of the service, and to
prevent its common purpose being frustrated through

the undue influence of the motive of pecuniary gain
upon the necessities or cupidity of the individual.

The difference between industry as it exists to-day
and a profession is, then, simple and unmistakable.
The essence of the former is that its only criterion is
the financial return which it offers to its shareholders.
The essence of the latter, is that, though men enter it
for the sake of livelihood, the measure of their success
is the service which they perform, not the gains which
they amass. They may, as in the case of a successful
doctor, grow rich; but the meaning of their profession,
both for themselves and for the public, is not that they
make money but that they make health, or safety, or
knowledge, or good government or good law. They
depend on it for their income, but they do not consider
that any conduct which increases their income is on
that account good. And while a boot-manufacturer who
retires with half a million is counted to have achieved
success, whether the boots which he made were of
leather or brown paper, a civil servant who did the
same would be impeached.

So, if they are doctors, they recognize that there are
certain kinds of conduct which cannot be practised,
however large the fee offered for them, because they
are unprofessional; if scholars and teachers, that it is
wrong to make money by deliberately deceiving the
public, as is done by makers of patent medicines, however much the public may clamor to be deceived; if
judges or public servants, that they must not increase
their incomes by selling justice for money; if soldiers,
that the service comes first, and their private inclina-

tions, even the reasonable preference of life to death,
second. Every country has its traitors, every army its
deserters, and every profession its blacklegs. To idealize
the professional spirit would be very absurd; it has its
sordid side, and, if it is to be fostered in industry, safe-
guards will be needed to check its excesses. But there
is all the difference between maintaining a standard
which is occasionally abandoned, and affirming as the
central truth of existence that there is no standard to
maintain. The meaning of a profession is that it makes
the traitors the exception, not as they are in industry,
the rule. It makes them the exception by upholding as
the criterion of success the end for which the profession,
whatever it may be, is carried on, and subordinating the
inclination, appetites and ambitions of individuals to
the rules of an organization which has as its object to
promote the performance of function.

There is no sharp line between the professions and
the industries. A hundred years ago the trade of teaching, which to-day is on the whole an honorable public
service, was rather a vulgar speculation upon public
credulity; if Mr. Squeers was a caricature, the Oxford
of Gibbon and Adam Smith was a solid port-fed reality;
no local authority could have performed one-tenth of
the duties which are carried out by a modern municipal
corporation every day, because there was no body of
public servants to perform them, and such as there were
took bribes. It is conceivable, at least, that some
branches of medicine might have developed on the lines
of industrial capitalism, with hospitals as factories,

doctors hired at competitive wages as their "hands," large dividends paid to shareholders by catering for the rich, and the poor, who do not offer a profitable market, supplied with an inferior service or with no service at all.

The idea that there is some mysterious difference between making munitions of war and firing them, between building schools and teaching in them when built, between providing food and providing health, which makes it at once inevitable and laudable that the former should be carried on with a single eye to pecuniary gain, while the latter are conducted by professional men who expect to be paid for service but who neither watch for windfalls nor raise their fees merely because there are more sick to be cured, more children to be taught, or more enemies to be resisted, is an illusion only less astonishing than that the leaders of industry should welcome the insult as an honor and wear their humiliation as a kind of halo. The work of making boots or building a house is in itself no more degrading than that of curing the sick or teaching the ignorant. It is as necessary and therefore as honorable. It should be at least equally bound by rules which have as their object to maintain the standards of professional service. It should be at least equally free from the vulgar subordination of moral standards to financial interests.

If industry is to be organized as a profession, two changes are requisite, one negative and one positive. The first, is that it should cease to be conducted by the agents of property-owners for the advantage of property-owners, and should be carried on, instead, for the service of the public. The second, is that, subject to rigorous public supervision, the responsibility for the maintenance of the service should rest upon the shoulders of those, from organizer and scientist to laborer, by whom, in effect, the work is conducted.

The first change is necessary because the conduct of industry for the public advantage is impossible as long as the ultimate authority over its management is vested in those whose only connection with it, and interest in it, is the pursuit of gain. As industry is at present organized, its profits and its control belong by law to that element in it which has least to do with its success. Under the joint-stock organization which has become normal in all the more important industries except agriculture, it is managed by the salaried agents of those by whom the property is owned. It is successful if it returns largs sums to shareholders, and unsuccessful if it does not. If an opportunity presents itself to increase dividends by practices which deteriorate the service or degrade the workers, the officials who administer industry act strictly within their duty if they seize it, for they are the servants of their employers, and their obligation to their employers is to provide dividends not to provide service. But the owners of the property are, *qua* property-owners functionless, not in the sense, of course, that the tools of which they are proprietors are not useful, but in the sense that since work and ownership are increasingly separated, the efficient use of the tools is not dependent on the maintenance of the proprietary rights exercised over them.

Of course there are many managing directors who both own capital and administer the business. But it is none the less the case that most shareholders in most large industries are normally shareholders and nothing more.

Nor is their economic interest identical, as is sometimes assumed, with that of the general public. A society is rich when material goods, including capital, are cheap, and human beings dear: indeed the word " riches " has no other meaning. The interest of those who own the property used in industry, though not, of course, of the managers who administer industry and who themselves are servants, and often very ill-paid servants at that, is that their capital should be dear and human beings cheap. Hence, if the industry is such as to yield a considerable return, or if one unit in the industry, owing to some special advantage, produces more cheaply than its neighbors, while selling at the same price, or if a revival of trade raises prices, or if supplies are controlled by one of the combines which are now the rule in many of the more important industries, the resulting surplus normally passes neither to the managers, nor to the other employees, nor to the public, but to the shareholders. Such an arrangement is preposterous in the literal sense of being the reverse of that which would be established by considerations of equity and common sense, and gives rise (among other things) to what is called " the struggle between labor and capital." The phrase is apposite, since it is as absurd as the relations of which it is intended to be a description. To deplore " ill-feeling " or to advocate

" harmony " between " labor and capital " is as rational
as to lament the bitterness between carpenters and ham-
mers or to promote a mission for restoring amity between mankind and its boots. The only significance of
these *clichés* is that their repetition tends to muffle their
inanity, even to the point of persuading sensible men
that capital " employs " labor, much as our pagan ancestors imagined that the other pieces of wood and iron,
which they deified in their day, sent their crops and won
their battles. When men have gone so far as to talk
as though their idols have come to life, it is time that
some one broke them. Labor consists of persons, capital of things. The only use of things is to be applied
to the service of persons. The business of persons is
to see that they are there to use, and that no more than
need be is paid for using them.

Thus the application to industry of the principle of
function involves an alteration of proprietary rights,
because those rights do not contribute, as they now are,
to the end which industry exists to serve. What gives
unity to any activity, what alone can reconcile the con-
flicting claims of the different groups engaged in it, is
the purpose for which it is carried on. If men have no
common goal it is no wonder that they should fall out
by the way, nor are they likely to be reconciled by a
redistribution of their provisions. If they are not content both to be servants, one or other must be master,
and it is idle to suppose that mastership can be held in
a state of suspense between the two. There can be a
division of functions between different grades of
workers, or between worker and consumer, and each can

have in his own sphere the authority needed to enable him to fill it. But there cannot be a division of functions between the worker and the owner who is owner and nothing else, for what function does such an owner perform? The provision of capital? Then pay him the sum needed to secure the use of his capital, but neither pay him more nor admit him to a position of authority over production for which merely as an owner he is not qualified. For this reason, while an equilibrium between worker and manager is possible, because both are workers, that which it is sought to establish between worker and owner is not. It is like the proposal of the Germans to negotiate with Belgium from Brussels. Their proposals may be excellent: but it is not evident why they are where they are, or how, since they do not contribute to production, they come to be putting forward proposals at all. As long as they are in territory where they have no business to be, their excellence as individuals will be overlooked in annoyance at the system which puts them where they are.

It is fortunate indeed, if nothing worse than this happens. For one way of solving the problem of the conflict of rights in industry is not to base rights on functions, as we propose, but to base them on force. It is to re-establish in some veiled and decorous form the institution of slavery, by making labor compulsory. In nearly all countries a concerted refusal to work has been made at one time or another a criminal offense. There are to-day parts of the world in which European capitalists, unchecked by any public opinion or authority independent of themselves, are free to impose almost what terms they please upon workmen of ignorant and helpless races. In those districts of America where capitalism still retains its primitive lawlessness, the same result appears to be produced upon immigrant workmen by the threat of violence.

In such circumstances the conflict of rights which finds expression in industrial warfare does not arise, because the rights of one party have been extinguished. The simplicity of the remedy is so attractive that it is not surprising that the Governments of industrial nations should coquet from time to time with the policy of compulsory arbitration. After all, it is pleaded, it is only analogous to the action of a supernational authority which should use its common force to prevent the outbreak of war. In reality, compulsory arbitration is the opposite of any policy which such an authority could pursue either with justice or with hope of success. For it takes for granted the stability of existing relationships and intervenes to adjust incidental disputes upon the assumption that their equity is recognized and their permanence desired. In industry, however, the equity of existing relationships is precisely the point at issue. A League of Nations which adjusted between a subject race and its oppressors, between Slavs and Magyars, or the inhabitants of what was once Prussian Poland and the Prussian Government, on the assumption that the subordination of Slavs to Magyars and Poles to Prussians was part of an unchangeable order, would rightly be resisted by all those who think liberty more precious than peace. A State which, in the name of peace, should make the concerted cessation of work a legal offense would be guilty of a similar betrayal of freedom. It would be solving the conflict of rights between those who own and those who work by abolishing the rights of those who work.

So here again, unless we are prepared to re-establish some form of forced labor, we reach an *impasse*. But it is an *impasse* only in so long as we regard the proprietary rights of those who own the capital used in industry as absolute and an end in themselves. If, instead of assuming that all property, merely because it is property, is equally sacred, we ask what is the *purpose* for which capital is used, what is its *function,* we shall realize that it is not an end but a means to an end, and that its function is to serve and assist (as the economists tell us) the labor of human beings, not the function of human beings to serve those who happen to own it. And from this truth two consequences follow. The first is that since capital is a thing, which ought to be used to help industry as a man may use a bicycle to get more quickly to his work, it ought, when it is employed, to be employed on the cheapest terms possible. The second is that those who own it should no more control production than a man who lets a house controls the meals which shall be cooked in the kitchen, or the man who lets a boat the speed at which the rowers shall pull. In other words, capital should always be got at cost price, which means, unless the State finds it wise, as it very well may, to own the capital used in certain industries, it should be paid the lowest interest for which it can be obtained, but should carry no right either to residuary dividends or to the control of industry.

There are, in theory, five ways by which the control of industry by the agents of private property-owners can be terminated. They may be expropriated without compensation. They may voluntarily surrender it. They may be frozen out by action on the part of the working *personnel,* which itself undertakes such functions, if any, as they have performed, and makes them superfluous by conducting production without their assistance. Their proprietary interest may be limited or attenuated to such a degree that they become mere *rentiers,* who are guaranteed a fixed payment analogous to that of the debenture-holder, but who receive no profits and bear no responsibility for the organization of industry. They may be bought out. The first alternative is exemplified by the historical confiscations of the past, such as, for instance, by the seizure of ecclesiastical property by the ruling classes of England, Scotland and most other Protestant states. The second has rarely, if ever, been tried—the nearest approach to it, perhaps, was the famous abdication of August 4th, 1789. The third is the method apparently contemplated by the building guilds which are now in process of formation in Great Britain. The fourth method of treating the capitalist is followed by the co-operative movement. It is also that proposed by the committee of employers and trade-unionists in the building industry over which Mr. Foster presided, and which proposed that employers should be paid a fixed salary, and a fixed rate of inter-

est on their capital, but that all surplus profits should
be pooled and administered by a central body representing employers and workers. The fifth has repeat-
edly been practised by municipalities, and somewhat
less often by national governments.

Which of these alternative methods of removing industry from the control of the property-owner is adopted
is a matter of expediency to be decided in each particular case. "Nationalization," therefore, which is sometimes advanced as the only method of extinguishing proprietary rights, is merely one species of a considerable
genus. It can be used, of course, to produce the desired
result. But there are some industries, at any rate, in
which nationalization is not necessary in order to bring
it about, and since it is at best a cumbrous process, when
other methods are possible, other methods should be
used. Nationalization is a means to an end, not an end
in itself. Properly conceived its object is not to establish state management of industry, but to remove the
dead hand of private ownership, when the private owner
has ceased to perform any positive function. It is un-
fortunate, therefore, that the abolition of obstructive
property rights, which is indispensable, should have
been identified with a single formula, which may be
applied with advantage in the special circumstances of
some industries, but need not necessarily be applied in
all. Ownership is not a right, but a bundle of rights,
and it is possible to strip them off piecemeal as well as
to strike them off simultaneously. The ownership of
capital involves, as we have said, three main claims; the
right to interest as the price of capital, the right to

profits, and the right to control, in virtue of which managers and workmen are the servants of shareholders. These rights in their fullest degree are not the invariable accompaniment of ownership, nor need they necessarily co-exist. The ingenuity of financiers long ago devised methods of grading stock in such a way that the ownership of some carries full control, while that of others does not, that some bear all the risk and are entitled to all the profits, while others are limited in respect to both. All are property, but not all carry proprietary rights of the same degree.

As long as the private ownership of industrial capital remains, the object of reformers should be to attenuate its influence by insisting that it shall be paid not more than a rate of interest fixed in advance, and that it should carry with it no right of control. In such circumstances the position of the ordinary shareholder would approximate to that of the owner of debentures; the property in the industry would be converted into a mortgage on its profits, while the control of its administration and all profits in excess of the minimum would remain to be vested elsewhere. So, of course, would the risks. But risks are of two kinds, those of the individual business and those of the industry. The former are much heavier than the latter, for though a coal mine is a speculative investment, coal mining is not, and as long as each business is managed as a separate unit, the payments made to shareholders must cover both. If the ownership of capital in each industry were unified, which does not mean centralized, those risks which are incidental to individual competition would be eliminated, and the credit of each unit would be that of the whole.

Such a change in the character of ownership would have three advantages. It would abolish the government of industry by property. It would end the payment of profits to functionless shareholders by turning them into creditors paid a fixed rate of interest. It would lay the only possible foundations for industrial peace by making it possible to convert industry into a profession carried on by all grades of workers for the service of the public, not for the gain of those who own capital. The organization which it would produce will be described, of course, as impracticable. It is interesting, therefore, to find it is that which experience has led practical men to suggest as a remedy for the disorders of one of the most important of national industries, that of building. The question before the Committee of employers and workmen, which issued last August a Report upon the Building Trade, was "Scientific Management and the Reduction of Costs."[1] These are not phrases which suggest an economic revolution; but it is something little short of a revolution that the signatories of the report propose. For, as soon as they came to grips with the problem, they found that it was impossible to handle it effectively without reconstituting the general fabric of industrial relationships which is its setting. Why is the service supplied by the industry ineffective? Partly because the workers do not give their full energies to the performance of their part in production.

[1] Reprinted in *The Industrial Council for the Building Industry.*

Why do they not give their best energies? Because of "the fear of unemployment, the disinclination of the operatives to make unlimited profit for private employers, the lack of interest evinced by operatives owing to their non-participation in control, inefficiency both managerial and operative." How are these psychological obstacles to efficiency to be counteracted? By increased supervision and speeding up, by the allurements of a premium bonus system, or the other devices by which men who are too ingenious to have imagination or moral insight would bully or cajole poor human nature into doing what—if only the systems they invent would let it!—it desires to do, simple duties and honest work? Not at all. By turning the building of houses into what teaching now is, and Mr. Squeers thought it could never be, an honorable profession.

"We believe," they write, "that the great task of our Industrial Council is to develop an entirely new system of industrial control by the members of the industry itself—the actual producers, whether by hand or brain, and to bring them into co-operation with the State as the central representative of the community whom they are organized to serve." Instead of unlimited profits, so "indispensable as an incentive to efficiency," the employer is to be paid a salary for his services as manager, and a rate of interest on his capital which is to be both fixed and (unless he fails to earn it through his own inefficiency) guaranteed; anything in excess of it, any "profits" in fact, which in other industries are distributed as dividends to shareholders, he is to surrender to a central fund to be administered by employers and workmen for the benefit of the industry as a whole. Instead of the financial standing of each firm being treated as an inscrutable mystery to the public, with the result that it is sometimes a mystery to itself, there is to be a system of public costing and audit, on the basis of which the industry will assume a collective liability for those firms which are shown to be competently managed. Instead of the workers being dismissed in slack times to struggle along as best they can, they are to be maintained from a fund raised by a levy on employers and administered by the trade unions. There is to be publicity as to costs and profits, open dealing and honest work and mutual helpfulness, instead of the competition which the nineteenth century regarded as an efficient substitute for them. " Capital " is not to " employ labor." Labor, which includes managerial labor, is to employ capital; and to employ it at the cheapest rate at which, in the circumstances of the trade, it can be got. If it employs it so successfully that there is a surplus when it has been fairly paid for its own services, then that surplus is not to be divided among shareholders, for, when they have been paid interest, they have been paid their due; it is to be used to equip the industry to provide still more effective service in the future.

So here we have the majority of a body of practical men, who care nothing for socialist theories, proposing to establish " organized Public Service in the Building Industry," recommending, in short, that their industry shall be turned into a profession. And they do it, it will be observed, by just that functional organization, just that conversion of full proprietary rights into a mortgage secured (as far as efficient firms are concerned) on the industry as a whole, just that transference of the control of production from the owner of capital to those whose business is production, which we saw is necessary if industry is to be organized for the performance of service, not for the pecuniary advantage of those who hold proprietary rights.   Their Report is of the first importance as offering a policy for attenuating private property in capital in the important group of industries in which private ownership, in one form or another, is likely for some considerable time to continue, and a valuable service would be rendered by any one who would work out in detail the application of its principle to other trades.

Not, of course, that this is the only way, or in highly capitalized industries the most feasible way, in which the change can be brought about. Had the movement against the control of production by property taken place before the rise of limited companies, in which ownership is separated from management, the transition to the organization of industry as a profession might also have taken place, as the employers and workmen in the building trade propose that it should, by limiting the rights of private ownership without abolishing it.   But that is not what has actually happened, and therefore the proposals of the building trade are not of universal application.   It is possible to retain private ownership in building and in industries like building, while changing its character, precisely because in building the employer is normally not merely an owner, but something else as well. He is a manager; that is, he is a workman. And because he is a workman, whose interests, and still more whose professional spirit as a workman may often outweigh his interests and merely financial spirit as an owner, he can form part of the productive organization of the industry, after his rights as an owner have been trimmed and limited.

But that dual position is abnormal, and in the highly organized industries is becoming more abnormal every year. In coal, in cotton, in ship-building, in many branches of engineering the owner of capital is not, as he is in building, an organizer or manager. His connection with the industry and interest in it is purely financial. He is an owner and nothing more. And because his interest is merely financial, so that his concern is dividends and production only as a means to dividends, he cannot be worked into an organization of industry which vests administration in a body representing all grades of producers, or producers and consumers together, for he has no purpose in common with them; so that while joint councils between workers and managers may succeed, joint councils between workers and owners or agents of owners, like most of the so-called Whitley Councils, will not, because the necessity for the mere owner is itself one of the points in dispute. The master builder, who owns the capital used, can be included, not *qua* capitalist, but *qua* builder, if he surrenders some of the rights of ownership, as the Building Industry Committee proposed that he should. But if the shareholder in a colliery or a shipyard abdicates the control and unlimited profits to which, *qua* capitalist, he is at present entitled, he abdicates everything that makes him what he is, and has no other standing in the industry. He cannot share, like the master builder, in its management, because he has no qualifications which would enable him to do so. His object is profit; and if industry is to become, as employers and workers in the building trade propose, an " organized public service," then its subordination to the shareholder whose object is profit, is, as they clearly see, precisely what must be eliminated. The master builders propose to give it up. They can do so because they have their place in the industry in virtue of their function as workmen. But if the shareholder gave it up, he would have no place at all.

Hence in coal mining, where ownership and management are sharply separated, the owners will not admit the bare possibility of any system in which the control of the administration of the mines is shared between the management and the miners. " I am authorized to state on behalf of the Mining Association," Lord Gainford, the chief witness on behalf of the mine-owners, informed the Coal Commission, " that if the owners are not to be left complete executive control they will decline to accept the responsibility for carrying on the industry." [1] So the mine-owners blow away in a sentence the whole body of plausible make-believe which rests on the idea that, while private ownership remains

[1] *Coal Industry Commission, Minutes of Evidence,* Vol. I, p. 2506.

unaltered, industrial harmony can be produced by the magic formula of joint control. And they are right. The representatives of workmen and shareholders, in mining and in other industries, can meet and negotiate and discuss. But joint administration of the shareholders' property by a body representing shareholders and workmen is impossible, because there is no purpose in common between them. For the only purpose which could unite all persons engaged in industry, and over-rule their particular and divergent interests, is the provision of service. And the object of shareholders, the whole significance and *métier* of industry to them, is not the provision of service but the provision of dividends.

In industries where management is divorced from ownership, as in most of the highly organized trades it is to-day, there is no obvious halfway house, therefore, between the retention of the present system and the complete extrusion of the capitalist from the control of production. The change in the character of ownership, which is necessary in order that coal or textiles and ship-building may be organized as professions for the service of the public, cannot easily spring from within. The stroke needed to liberate them from the control of the property-owner must come from without. In theory it might be struck by action on the part of organized workers, who would abolish residuary profits and the right of control by the mere procedure of refusing to work as long as they were maintained, on the historical analogy offered by peasants who have destroyed predatory property in the past by declining to pay its dues and admit its government, in which case Parliament would intervene only to register the community's assent to the *fait accompli*. In practice, however, the conditions of modern industry being what they are, that course, apart from its other disadvantages, is so unlikely to be attempted, or, if attempted, to succeed, that it can be neglected. The alternative to it is that the change in the character of property should be affected by legislation in virtue of which the rights of ownership in an industry are bought out simultaneously.

In either case, though the procedure is different, the result of the change, once it is accomplished, is the same. Private property in capital, in the sense of the right to profits and control, is abolished. What remains of it is, at most, a mortgage in favor of the previous proprietors, a dead leaf which is preserved, though the sap of industry no longer feeds it, as long as it is not thought worth while to strike it off. And since the capital needed to maintain and equip a modern industry could not be provided by any one group of workers, even were it desirable on other grounds that they should step completely into the position of the present owners, the complex of rights which constitutes ownership remains to be shared between them and whatever organ may act on behalf of the general community. The former, for example, may be the heir of the present owners as far as the control of the routine and administration of industry is concerned: the latter may succeed to their right to dispose of residuary profits. The elements composing property, have, in fact, to be disentangled: and the fact that to-day, under the common name of ownership, several different powers are vested in identical hands, must not be allowed to obscure the probability that, once private property in capital has been abolished, it may be expedient to re-allocate those powers in detail as well as to transfer them *en bloc*.

The essence of a profession is, as we have suggested, that its members organize themselves for the performance of function. It is essential therefore, if industry is to be professionalized, that the abolition of functionless property should not be interpreted to imply a continuance under public ownership of the absence of responsibility on the part of the *personnel* of industry, which is the normal accompaniment of private ownership working through the wage-system. It is the more important to emphasize that point, because such an implication has sometimes been conveyed in the past by some of those who have presented the case for some such change in the character of ownership as has been urged above. The name consecrated by custom to the transformation of property by public and external action is nationalization. But nationalization is a word which is neither very felicitous nor free from ambiguity. Properly used, it means merely ownership by a body representing the nation. But it has come in practice to be used as equivalent to a particular method of administration, under which officials employed by the State step into the position of the present directors of industry, and exercise all the power which they exercised. So those who desire to maintain the system under which industry is carried on, not as a profession

serving the public, but for the advantage of shareholders, attack nationalization on the ground that state
management is necessarily inefficient, and tremble with
apprehension whenever they post a letter in a letter-box;
and those who desire to change it reply that state services are efficient and praise God whenever they use a
telephone; as though either private or public administration had certain peculiar and unalterable characteristics, instead of depending for its quality, like an army
or railway company or school, and all other undertakings, public and private alike, not on whether those
who conduct it are private officials or state officials, but
on whether they are properly trained for their work
and can command the good will and confidence of their
subordinates.

The arguments on both sides are ingenious, but in
reality nearly all of them are beside the point. The
merits of nationalization do not stand or fall with the
efficiency or inefficiency of existing state departments
as administrators of industry. For nationalization,
which means public ownership, is compatible with several different types of management. The constitution
of the industry may be " unitary," as is (for example)
that of the post-office. Or it may be " federal," as was
that designed by Mr. Justice Sankey for the Coal Industry. Administration may be centralized or decentralized. The authorities to whom it is intrusted may
be composed of representatives of the consumers, or of
representatives of professional associations, or of state
officials, or of all three in several different proportions.
Executive work may be placed in the hands of civil

servants, trained, recruited and promoted as in the existing state departments, or a new service may be created with a procedure and standards of its own. It may be subject to Treasury control, or it may be financially autonomous. The problem is, in fact, of a familiar, though difficult, order. It is one of constitution-making.

It is commonly assumed by controversialists that the organization and management of a nationalized industry must, for some undefined reason, be similar to that of the post-office. One might as reasonably suggest that the pattern exemplar of private enterprise must be the Steel Corporation or the Imperial Tobacco Company. The administrative systems obtaining in a society which has nationalized its foundation industries will, in fact, be as various as in one that resigns them to private ownership; and to discuss their relative advantages without defining what particular type of each is the subject of reference is to-day as unhelpful as to approach a modern political problem in terms of the Aristotelian classification of constitutions. The highly abstract dialectics as to " enterprise," " initiative," " bureaucracy," " red tape," " democratic control," " state management," which fill the press of countries occupied with industrial problems, really belong to the dark ages of economic thought. The first task of the student, whatever his personal conclusions, is, it may be suggested, to contribute what he can to the restoration of sanity by insisting that instead of the argument being conducted with the counters of a highly inflated and rapidly depreciating verbal currency, the exact situation.

in so far as is possible, shall be stated as it is; uncertainties (of which there are many) shall be treated as uncertain, and the precise meaning of alternative proposals shall be strictly defined. Not the least of the merits of Mr. Justice Sankey's report was that, by stating in great detail the type of organization which he recommended for the Coal Industry, he imparted a new precision and reality into the whole discussion. Whether his conclusions are accepted or not, it is from the basis of clearly defined proposals such as his that the future discussion of these problems must proceed. It may not find a solution. It will at least do something to create the temper in which alone a reasonable solution can be sought.

Nationalization, then, is not an end, but a means to an end, and when the question of ownership has been settled the question of administration remains for solution. As a means it is likely to be indispensable in those industries in which the rights of private proprietors cannot easily be modified without the action of the State, just as the purchase of land by county councils is a necessary step to the establishment of small holders, when landowners will not voluntarily part with their property for the purpose. But the object in purchasing land is to establish small holders, not to set up farms administered by state officials; and the object of nationalizing mining or railways or the manufacture of steel should not be to establish any particular form of state management, but to release those who do constructive work from the control of those whose sole interest is pecuniary gain, in order that they may be free to apply their energies to the true purpose of industry, which is the provision of service, not the provision of dividends. When the transference of property has taken place, it will probably be found that the necessary provision for the government of industry will involve not merely the freedom of the producers to produce, but the creation of machinery through which the consumer, for whom he produces, can express his wishes and criticize the way in which they are met, as at present he normally cannot. But that is the second stage in the process of reorganizing industry for the performance of function, not the first. The first is to free it from subordination to the pecuniary interests of the owner of property, because they are the magnetic pole which sets all the compasses wrong, and which causes industry, however swiftly it may progress, to progress in the wrong direction.

Nor does this change in the character of property involve a breach with the existing order so sharp as to be impracticable. The phraseology of political controversy continues to reproduce the conventional antitheses of the early nineteenth century; "private enterprise" and "public ownership" are still contrasted with each other as light with darkness or darkness with light. But, in reality, behind the formal shell of the traditional legal system the elements of a new body of relationship have already been prepared, and find piecemeal application through policies devised, not by socialists, but by men who repeat the formulæ of individualism, at the very moment when they are undermining it. The Esch-Cummins Act in America, the

Act establishing a Ministry of Transport in England,
Sir Arthur Duckham's scheme for the organization of
the coal mines, the proposals with regard to the coal industry of the British Government itself, appear to have
the common characteristic of retaining private ownership in name, while attenuating it in fact, by placing
its operators under the supervision, accompanied sometimes by a financial guarantee, of a public authority.
Schemes of this general character appear, indeed, to be
the first instinctive reaction produced by the discovery
that private enterprise is no longer functioning effectively; it is probable that they possess certain merits of
a technical order analogous to those associated with the
amalgamation of competing firms into a single combination.   It is questionable, however, whether the compromise which they represent is permanently tenable.
What, after all, it may be asked, are the advantages of
private ownership when it has been pared down to the
point which policies of this order propose?   May not
the " owner " whose rights they are designed to protect
not unreasonably reply to their authors, " Thank you
for nothing "?   Individual enterprise has its merits:
so also, perhaps, has public ownership.   But, by the time
these schemes have done with it, not much remains of
" the simple and obvious system of natural liberty,"
while their inventors are precluded from appealing to
the motives which are emphasized by advocates of nationalization.   It is one thing to be an entrepreneur
with a world of adventure and unlimited profits—if
they can be achieved—before one.   It is quite another
to be a director of a railway company or coal corpora-

tion with a minimum rate of profit guaranteed by the State, and a maximum rate of profit which cannot be exceeded. Hybrids are apt to be sterile. It may be questioned whether, in drawing the teeth of private capitalism, this type of compromise does not draw out most of its virtues as well.

So, when a certain stage of economic development has been reached, private ownership, by the admission of its defenders, can no longer be tolerated in the only form in which it is free to display the characteristic, and quite genuine, advantages for the sake of which it used to be defended. And, as step by step it is whittled down by tacit concessions to the practical necessity of protecting the consumer, or eliminating waste, or meeting the claims of the workers, public ownership becomes, not only on social grounds, but for reasons of economic efficiency, the alternative to a type of private ownership which appears to carry with it few rights of ownership and to be singularly devoid of privacy. Inevitably and unfortunately the change must be gradual. But it should be continuous. When, as in the last few years, the State has acquired the ownership of great masses of industrial capital, it should retain it, instead of surrendering it to private capitalists, who protest at once that it will be managed so inefficiently that it will not pay and managed so efficiently that it will undersell them. When estates are being broken up and sold, as they are at present, public bodies should enter the market and acquire them. Most important of all, the ridiculous barrier, inherited from an age in which municipal corporations were corrupt oligarchies, which at present prevents England's Local Authorities from acquiring property in land and industrial capital, except for purposes specified by Act of Parliament, should be abolished, and they should be free to undertake such services as the citizens may desire. The objection to public ownership, in so far as it is intelligent, is in reality largely an objection to over-centralization. But the remedy for over-centralization, is not the maintenance of functionless property in private hands, but the decentralized ownership of public property, and when Birmingham and Manchester and Leeds are the little republics which they should be, there is no reason to anticipate that they will tremble at a whisper from Whitehall.

These things should be done steadily and continuously quite apart from the special cases like that of the mines and railways, where the private ownership of capital is stated by the experts to have been responsible for intolerable waste, or the manufacture of ornaments and alcoholic liquor, which are politically and socially too dangerous to be left in private hands. They should be done not in order to establish a single form of bureaucratic management, but in order to release the industry from the domination of proprietary interests, which, whatever the form of management, are not merely troublesome in detail but vicious in principle, because they divert it from the performance of function to the acquisition of gain. If at the same time private ownership is shaken, as recently it has been, by action on the part of particular groups of workers, so much the better. There are more ways of killing a cat than drowning it in cream, and it is all the more likely to choose the cream if they are explained to it. But the two methods are complementary, not alternative, and the attempt to found rival schools on an imaginary incompatibility between them is a bad case of the *odium sociologicum* which afflicts reformers.

EIGHT

THE " VICIOUS CIRCLE "

♦

WHAT form of management should replace the administration of industry by the agents of shareholders?
What is most likely to hold it to its main purpose, and
to be least at the mercy of predatory interests and functionless supernumeraries, and of the alternations of
sullen dissatisfaction and spasmodic revolt which at
present distract it? Whatever the system upon which
industry is administered, one thing is certain. Its economic processes and results must be public, because only
if they are public can it be known whether the service
of industry is vigilant, effective and honorable, whether
its purpose is being realized and its function carried
out. The defense of secrecy in business resembles the
defense of adulteration on the ground that it is a legitimate weapon of competition; indeed it has even less
justification than that famous doctrine, for the condition
of effective competition is publicity, and one motive for
secrecy is to prevent it.

Those who conduct industry at the present time and
who are most emphatic that, as the Duke of Wellington
said of the unreformed House of Commons, they " have
never read or heard of any measure up to the present
moment which can in any degree satisfy the mind " that
the method of conducting it can in any way be improved, are also those apparently who, with some honor-

able exceptions, are most reluctant that the full facts about it should be known. And it is crucial that they should be known. It is crucial not only because, in the present ignorance of the real economic situation, all industrial disagreements tend inevitably to be battles in the dark, in which " ignorant armies clash by night," but because, unless there is complete publicity as to profits and costs, it is impossible to form any judgment either of the reasonableness of the prices which are charged or of the claims to remuneration of the different parties engaged in production. For balance sheets, with their opportunities for concealing profits, give no clear light upon the first, and no light at all upon the second. And so, when the facts come out, the public is aghast at revelations which show that industry is conducted with bewildering financial extravagance. If the full facts had been published, as they should have been, quarter by quarter, these revelations would probably not have been made at all, because publicity itself would have been an antiseptic and there would have been nothing sensational to reveal.

The events of the last few years are a lesson which should need no repetition. The Government, surprised at the price charged for making shells at a time when its soldiers were ordered by Headquarters not to fire more than a few rounds per day, whatever the need for retaliation, because there were not more than a few to fire, establishes a costing department to analyze the estimates submitted by manufacturers and to compare them, item by item, with the costs in its own factories. It finds that, through the mere pooling of knowledge,

" some of the reductions made in the price of shells and similar munitions," as the Chartered Accountant employed by the Department tells us, " have been as high as 50% of the original price." The household consumer grumbles at the price of coal. For once in a way, amid a storm of indignation from influential persons engaged in the industry, the facts are published. And what do they show? That, after 2/6 has been added to the already high price of coal because the poorer mines are alleged not to be paying their way, 21% of the output examined by the Commission was produced at a profit of 1/- to 3/- per ton, 32% at a profit of 3/- to 5/-, 13% at a profit of 5/- to 7/-, and 14% at a profit of 7/- per ton and over, while the profits of distributors in London alone amount in the aggregate to over £500,000, and the co-operative movement, which aims not at profit, but at service, distributes household coal at a cost of from 2/- to 4/- less per ton than is charged by the coal trade ! [1]

" But these are exceptions." They may be. It is possible that in the industries, in which, as the recent Committee on Trusts has told us, " powerful Combinations or Consolidations of one kind or another are in a position effectively to control output and prices," not only costs are cut to the bare minimum but profits are inconsiderable. But then why insist on this humiliating tradition of secrecy with regard to them, when every one who uses their products, and every one who renders honest service to production, stands to gain by publicity? If industry is to become a profession, whatever its man-

[1] *Coal Industry Commission, Minutes of Evidence*, pp. 9261-9.

agement, the first of its professional rules should be, as Sir John Mann told the Coal Commission, that "all cards should be placed on the table." If it were the duty of a Public Department to publish quarterly exact returns as to costs of production and profits in all the firms throughout an industry, the gain in mere productive efficiency, which should appeal to our enthusiasts for output, would be considerable; for the organization whose costs were least would become the standard with which all other types of organization would be compared. The gain in *morale,* which is also, absurd though it may seem, a condition of efficiency, would be incalculable. For industry would be conducted in the light of day. Its costs, necessary or unnecessary, the distribution of the return to it, reasonable or capricious, would be a matter of common knowledge. It would be held to its purpose by the mere impossibility of persuading those who make its products or those who consume them to acquiesce, as they acquiesce now, in expenditure which is meaningless because it has contributed nothing to the service which the industry exists to perform.

The organization of industry as a profession does not involve only the abolition of functionless property, and the maintenance of publicity as the indispensable condition of a standard of professional honor. It implies also that those who perform its work should undertake that its work is performed effectively. It means that they should not merely be held to the service of the public by fear of personal inconvenience or penalties, but that they should treat the discharge of professional responsibilities as an obligation attaching not only to a small *élite* of intellectuals, managers or " bosses," who perform the technical work of " business management," but as implied by the mere entry into the industry and as resting on the corporate consent and initiative of the rank and file of workers. It is precisely, indeed, in the degree to which that obligation is interpreted as attaching to all workers, and not merely to a select class, that the difference between the existing industrial order, collectivism and the organization of industry as a profession resides. The first involves the utilization of human beings for the purpose of private gain; the second their utilization for the purpose of public service; the third the association in the service of the public of their professional pride, solidarity and organization.

The difference in administrative machinery between the second and third might not be considerable. Both involve the drastic limitation or transference to the public of the proprietary rights of the existing owners of industrial capital. Both would necessitate machinery for bringing the opinion of the consumers to bear upon the service supplied them by the industry. The difference consists in the manner in which the obligations of the producer to the public are conceived. He may either be the executant of orders transmitted to him by its agents; or he may, through his organization, himself take a positive part in determining what those orders should be. In the former case he is responsible for his own work, but not for anything else. If he hews his stint of coal, it is no business of his whether the pit is a failure; if he puts in the normal number of rivets, he disclaims all further interest in the price or the seaworthiness of the ship. In the latter his function embraces something more than the performance of the specialized piece of work allotted to him. It includes also a responsibility for the success of the undertaking as a whole. And since responsibility is impossible without power, his position would involve at least so much power as is needed to secure that he can affect in practice the conduct of the industry. It is this collective liability for the maintenance of a certain quality of service which is, indeed, the distinguishing feature of a profession. It is compatible with several different kinds of government, or indeed, when the unit of production is not a group, but an individual, with hardly any government at all. What it does involve is that the individual, merely by entering the profession should have committed himself to certain obligations in respect of its conduct, and that the professional organization, whatever it may be, should have sufficient power to enable it to maintain them.

The demand for the participation of the workers in the control of industry is usually advanced in the name of the producer, as a plea for economic freedom or industrial democracy. "Political freedom," writes the Final Report of the United States Commission of Industrial Relations, which was presented in 1916, " can exist only where there is industrial freedom. . . . There are now within the body of our Republic industrial communities which are virtually Principalities, oppressive to those dependent upon them for a livelihood and a dreadful menace to the peace and welfare of the nation." The vanity of Englishmen may soften the shadows and heighten the lights. But the concentration of authority is too deeply rooted in the very essence of Capitalism for differences in the degree of the arbitrariness with which it is exercised to be other than trivial. The control of a large works does, in fact, confer a kind of private jurisdiction in matters concerning the life and livelihood of the workers, which, as the United States' Commission suggests, may properly be described as "industrial feudalism." It is not easy to understand how the traditional liberties of Englishmen are compatible with an organization of industry which, except in so far as it has been qualified by law or trade unionism, permits populations almost as large as those of some famous cities of the past to be controlled in their rising up and lying down, in their work, economic opportunities, and social life by the decisions of a Committee of half-a-dozen Directors.

The most conservative thinkers recognize that the present organization of industry is intolerable in the sacrifice of liberty which it entails upon the producer. But each effort which he makes to emancipate himself is met by a protest that if the existing system is incompatible with freedom, it at least secures efficient service, and that efficient service is threatened by movements which aim at placing a greater measure of industrial control in the hands of the workers. The attempt to drive a wedge between the producer and the consumer is obviously the cue of all the interests which are conscious that by themselves they are unable to hold back the flood. It is natural, therefore, that during the last few months they should have concentrated their efforts upon representing that every advance in the demands and in the power of any particular group of workers is a new imposition upon the general body of the public. Eminent persons, who are not obviously producing more than they consume, explain to the working classes that unless they produce more they must consume less. Highly syndicated combinations warn the public against the menace of predatory syndicalism. The owners of mines and minerals, in their new rôle as protectors of the poor, lament the " selfishness " of the miners, as though nothing but pure philanthropy had hitherto caused profits and royalties to be reluctantly accepted by themselves.

The assumption upon which this body of argument rests is simple. It is that the existing organization of industry is the safeguard of productive efficiency, and that from every attempt to alter it the workers themselves lose more as consumers than they can gain as producers. The world has been drained of its wealth and demands abundance of goods. The workers demand a larger income, greater leisure, and a more secure and dignified status. These two demands, it is argued, are contradictory. For how can the consumer be supplied with cheap goods, if, as a worker, he insists on higher wages and shorter hours? And how can the worker secure these conditions, if as a consumer, he demands cheap goods? So industry, it is thought, moves in a vicious circle of shorter hours and higher wages and less production, which in time must mean longer hours and lower wages; and every one receives less, because every one demands more.

The picture is plausible, but it is fallacious. It is fallacious not merely in its crude assumption that a rise in wages necessarily involves an increase in costs, but for another and more fundamental reason. In reality the cause of economic confusion is not that the demands of producer and consumer meet in blunt opposition; for, if they did, their incompatibility, when they were incompatible, would be obvious, and neither could deny his responsibility to the other, however much he might seek to evade it. It is that they do not, but that, as industry is organized to-day, what the worker foregoes the general body of consumers does not necessarily gain, and what the consumer pays the general body of workers does not necessarily receive. If the circle is vicious, its vice is not that it is closed, but that it is always half open, so that part of production leaks away in consumption which adds nothing to productive energies, and that the producer, because he knows this, does not fully use even the productive energy which he commands.

It is the consciousness of this leak which sets every one at cross purposes. No conceivable system of industrial organization can secure industrial peace, if by " peace " is meant a complete absence of disagreement. What could be secured would be that disagreements should not flare up into a beacon of class warfare. If every member of a group puts something into a common pool on condition of taking something out, they may still quarrel about the size of the shares, as children quarrel over cake; but if the total is known and the claims admitted, that is all they can quarrel about, and, since they all stand on the same footing, any one who holds out for more than his fellows must show some good reason why he should get it. But in industry the claims are not all admitted, for those who put nothing in demand to take something out; both the total to be divided and the proportion in which the division takes place are sedulously concealed; and those who preside over the distribution of the pool and control what is paid out of it have a direct interest in securing as large a share as possible for themselves and in allotting as small a share as possible to others. If one contributor takes less, so far from it being evident that the gain will go to some one who has put something in and has as good a right as himself, it may go to some one who has put in nothing and has no right at all. If another claims more, he may secure it, without plundering a fellow-worker, at the expense of a sleeping partner who is believed to plunder both. In practice, since there is no clear principle determining what they ought to take, both take all that they can get.

In such circumstances denunciations of the producer for exploiting the consumer miss the mark. They are inevitably regarded as an economic version of the military device used by armies which advance behind a screen of women and children, and then protest at the brutality of the enemy in shooting non-combatants. They are interpreted as evidence, not that a section of the producers are exploiting the remainder, but that a minority of property-owners, which is in opposition to both, can use its economic power to make efforts directed against those who consume much and produce little rebound on those who consume little and produce much. And the grievance, of which the Press makes so much, that some workers may be taking too large a share compared with others, is masked by the much greater grievance, of which it says nothing whatever, that some idlers take any share at all. The abolition of payments which are made without any corresponding economic service is thus one of the indispensable conditions both of economic efficiency and industrial peace, because their existence prevents different classes of workers from restraining each other, by uniting them all against the common enemy. Either the principle of industry is that of function, in which case slack work is only less immoral than no work at all; or it is that of grab, in which case there is no morality in the matter. But it cannot be both. And it is useless either for property-owners or for Governments to lament the mote in the eye of the trade unions as long as, by insisting on the maintenance of functionless property, they decline to remove the beam in their own.

The truth is that only workers can prevent the abuse of power by workers, because only workers are recognized as possessing any title to have their claims considered. And the first step to preventing the exploitation of the consumer by the producer is simple. It is to turn all men into producers, and thus to remove the temptation for particular groups of workers to force their claims at the expense of the public, by removing the valid excuse that such gains as they may get are taken from those who at present have no right to them, because they are disproportionate to service or obtained for no service at all.   Indeed, if work were the only title to payment, the danger of the community being exploited by highly organized groups of producers would largely disappear.   For, when no payments were made to non-producers, there would be no debatable ground for which to struggle, and it would become evident that if any one group of producers took more, another must put up with less.

Under such conditions a body of workers who used their strong strategic position to extort extravagant terms for themselves at the expense of their fellow-workers might properly be described as exploiting the community.   But at present such a statement is meaningless.   It is meaningless because before the community can be exploited the community must exist, and its existence in the sphere of economics is to-day not a fact but only an aspiration.   The procedure by which, whenever any section of workers advance demands which are regarded as inconvenient by their masters, they are denounced as a band of anarchists who are preying on the public may be a convenient weapon in an emergency, but, once it is submitted to analysis, it is logically self-destructive.   It has been applied within recent years, to the postmen, to the engineers, to the policemen, to the miners and to the railway men, a population with their dependents, of some eight million persons; and in the case of the last two the whole body of organized labor made common cause with those of whose exorbitant demands it was alleged to be the victim.   But when these workers and their sympathizers are deducted, what is " the community " which remains? It is a naïve arithmetic which produces a total by subtracting one by one all the items which compose it; and the art which discovers the public interest by eliminating the interests of successive sections of the public smacks of the rhetorician rather than of the statesman.

The truth is that at present it is idle to seek to resist the demands of any group of workers by appeals to " the interests of society," because to-day, as long as the economic plane alone is considered, there is not one society but two, which dwell together in uneasy juxtaposition, like Sinbad and the Old Man of the Sea, but which in spirit, in ideals, and in economic interest, are worlds asunder. There is the society of those who live by labor, whatever their craft or profession, and the society of those who live on it. All the latter cannot command the sacrifices or the loyalty which are due to the former, for they have no title which will bear inspection. The instinct to ignore that tragic division instead of ending it is amiable, and sometimes generous. But it is a sentimentality which is like the morbid optimism of the consumptive who dares not admit even to himself the virulence of his disease. As long as the division exists, the general body of workers, while it may suffer from the struggles of any one group within it, nevertheless supports them by its sympathy, because all are interested in the results of the contest carried on by each. Different sections of workers will exercise mutual restraint only when the termination of the struggle leaves them face to face with each other, and not as now, with the common enemy. The ideal of a united society in which no one group uses its power to encroach upon the standards of another is, in short, unattainable, except through the preliminary abolition of functionless property.

Those to whom a leisure class is part of an immutable order without which civilization is inconceivable, dare not admit, even to themselves, that the world is poorer, not richer, because of its existence. So, when, as now it is important that productive energy should be fully used, they stamp and cry, and write to *The Times* about the necessity for increased production, though all the time they themselves, their way of life and expenditure, and their very existence as a leisure class, are among the causes why production is not increased. In all their economic plans they make one reservation, that, however necessitous the world may be, it shall still support *them*. But men who work do not make that reservation, nor is there any reason why they should; and appeals to them to produce more wealth because the public needs it usually fall upon deaf ears, even when such appeals are not involved in the ignorance and misapprehensions which often characterize them.

For the workman is not the servant of the consumer, for whose sake greater production is demanded, but of shareholders, whose primary aim is dividends, and to whom all production, however futile or frivolous, so long as it yields dividends, is the same. It is useless to urge that he should produce more wealth for the community, unless at the same time he is assured that it is the community which will benefit in proportion as more wealth is produced. If every unnecessary charge upon coal-getting had been eliminated, it would be reasonable that the miners should set a much needed example by refusing to extort better terms for themselves at the expense of the public. But there is no reason why they should work for lower wages or longer hours as long as those who are to-day responsible for the management of the industry conduct it with "the extravagance and waste" stigmatized by the most eminent official witness before the Coal Commission, or why the consumer should grumble at the rapacity of the miner as long as he allows himself to be mulcted by swollen profits, the costs of an ineffective organization, and unnecessary payments to superfluous middlemen.

If to-day the miner or any other workman produces more, he has no guarantee that the result will be lower prices rather than higher dividends and larger royalties, any more than, as a workman, he can determine the quality of the wares which his employer supplies to customers, or the price at which they are sold. Nor, as long as he is directly the servant of a profit-making company, and only indirectly the servant of the community, can any such guarantee be offered him. It can be offered only in so far as he stands in an immediate and direct relation to the public for whom industry is carried on, so that, when all costs have been met, any surplus will pass to it, and not to private individuals. It will be accepted only in so far as the workers in each industry are not merely servants executing orders, but themselves have a collective responsibility for the character of the service, and can use their organizations not merely to protect themselves against exploitation, but to make positive contributions to the administration and development of their industry.

NINE

THE CONDITION OF EFFICIENCY

◆

THUS it is not only for the sake of the producers, on whom the old industrial order weighed most heavily, that a new industrial order is needed. It is needed for the sake of the consumers, because the ability on which the old industrial order prided itself most and which is flaunted most as an argument against change, the ability to serve them effectively, is itself visibly breaking down. It is breaking down at what was always its most vulnerable point, the control of the human beings whom, with characteristic indifference to all but their economic significance, it distilled for its own purposes into an abstraction called " Labor." The first symptom of its collapse is what the first symptom of economic collapses has usually been in the past—the failure of customary stimuli to evoke their customary response in human effort.

Till that failure is recognized and industry reorganized so that new stimuli may have free play, the collapse will not correct itself, but, doubtless with spasmodic revivals and flickerings of energy, will continue and accelerate. The cause of it is simple. It is that those whose business it is to direct economic activity are increasingly incapable of directing the men upon whom economic activity depends. The fault is not that of individuals, but of a system, of Industrialism itself.

During the greater part of the nineteenth century industry was driven by two forces, hunger and fear, and the employer commanded them both. He could grant or withhold employment as he pleased. If men revolted against his terms he could dismiss them, and if they were dismissed what confronted them was starvation or the workhouse. Authority was centralized; its instruments were passive; the one thing which they dreaded was unemployment. And since they could neither prevent its occurrence nor do more than a little to mitigate its horrors when it occurred, they submitted to a discipline which they could not resist, and industry pursued its course through their passive acquiescence in a power which could crush them individually if they attempted to oppose it.

That system might be lauded as efficient or denounced as inhuman. But, at least, as its admirers were never tired of pointing out, it worked. And, like the Prussian State, which alike in its virtues and deficiencies it not a little resembled, as long as it worked it survived denunciations of its methods, as a strong man will throw off a disease. But to-day it is ceasing to have even the qualities of its defects. It is ceasing to be efficient. It no longer secures the ever-increasing output of wealth which it offered in its golden prime, and which enabled it to silence criticism by an imposing spectacle of material success. Though it still works, it works unevenly, amid constant friction and jolts and stoppages, without the confidence of the public and without full confidence even in itself, a tyrant who must intrigue and cajole where formerly he commanded, a gaoler who, if not yet deprived of whip, dare only administer moderate chastisement, and who, though he still protests that he alone can keep the treadmill moving and get the corn ground, is compelled to surrender so much of his authority as to make it questionable whether he is worth his keep. For the instruments through which Capitalism exercised discipline are one by one being taken from it. It cannot pay what wages it likes or work what hours it likes. In well-organized industries the power of arbitrary dismissal, the very center of its authority, is being shaken, because men will no longer tolerate a system which makes their livelihood dependent on the caprices of an individual. In all industries alike the time is not far distant when the dread of starvation can no longer be used to cow dissatisfied workers into submission, because the public will no longer allow involuntary unemployment to result in starvation.

And if Capitalism is losing its control of men's bodies, still more has it lost its command of their minds. The product of a civilization which regarded " the poor " as instruments, at worst of the luxuries, at best of the virtues, of the rich, its psychological foundation fifty years ago was an ignorance in the mass of mankind which led them to reverence as wisdom the very follies of their masters, and an almost animal incapacity for responsibility. Education and experience have destroyed the passivity which was the condition of the perpetuation of industrial government in the hands of an oligarchy of private capitalists. The workman of to-day has as little belief in the intellectual superiority of many of those who direct industry as he has in the morality of the system. It appears to him to be not only oppressive, but wasteful, unintelligent and inefficient. In the light of his own experience in the factory and the mine, he regards the claim of the capitalist to be the self-appointed guardian of public interests as a piece of sanctimonious hypocrisy. For he sees every day that efficiency is sacrificed to shortsighted financial interests; and while as a man he is outraged by the inhumanity of the industrial order, as a professional who knows the difference between good work and bad he has a growing contempt at once for its misplaced parsimony and its misplaced extravagance, for the whole apparatus of adulteration, advertisement and quackery which seems inseparable from the pursuit of profit as the main standard of industrial success.

So Capitalism no longer secures strenuous work by fear, for it is ceasing to be formidable. And it cannot secure it by respect, for it has ceased to be respected. And the very victories by which it seeks to reassert its waning prestige are more disastrous than defeats. Employers may congratulate themselves that they have maintained intact their right to freedom of management, or opposed successfully a demand for public ownership, or broken a movement for higher wages and shorter hours. But what is success in a trade dispute or in a political struggle is often a defeat in the workshop: the workmen may have lost, but it does not follow that their employers, still less that the public, which is principally composed of workmen, have won. For the object of industry is to produce goods, and to produce them at the lowest cost in human effort.

But there is no alchemy which will secure efficient production from the resentment or distrust of men who feel contempt for the order under which they work. It is a commonplace that credit is the foundation of industry.   But credit is a matter of psychology, and the workman has his psychology as well as the capitalist. If confidence is necessary to the investment of capital, confidence is not less necessary to the effective performance of labor by men whose sole livelihood depends upon it.   If they are not yet strong enough to impose their will, they are strong enough to resist when their masters would impose theirs. They may work rather than strike. But they will work to escape dismissal, not for the greater glory of a system in which they do not believe; and, if they are dismissed, those who take their place will do the same.

That this is one cause of a low output has been stated both by employers and workers in the building industry, and by the representatives of the miners before the Coal Commission.   It was reiterated with impressive emphasis by Mr. Justice Sankey. Nor is it seriously contested by employers themselves. What else, indeed, do their repeated denunciations of " restriction of output " mean except that they have failed to organize industry so as to secure the efficient service which it is their special function to provide?   Nor is it appropriate to the situation to indulge in full-blooded denunciations of the " selfishness " of the working classes.   " To draw an indictment against a whole nation " is a procedure which is as impossible in industry as it is in politics. Institutions must be adapted to human nature, not

human nature to institutions. If the effect of the industrial system is such that a large and increasing number
of ordinary men and women find that it offers them no
adequate motive for economic effort, it is mere pedantry
to denounce men and women instead of amending the
system.

Thus the time has come when absolutism in industry
may still win its battles, but loses the campaign, and
loses it on the very ground of economic efficiency which
was of its own selection. In the period of transition,
while economic activity is distracted by the struggle between those who have the name and habit of power, but
no longer the full reality of it, and those who are daily
winning more of the reality of power but are not yet
its recognized repositories, it is the consumer who
suffers. He has neither the service of docile obedience,
nor the service of intelligent co-operation. For slavery
will work—as long as the slaves will let it; and freedom
will work when men have learned to be free; but what
will not work is a combination of the two. So the
public goes short of coal not only because of the technical deficiencies of the system under which it is raised
and distributed, but because the system itself has lost
its driving force—because the coal owners can no longer
persuade the miners into producing more dividends for
them and more royalties for the owners of minerals,
while the public cannot appeal to them to put their
whole power into serving itself, because it has chosen
that they should be the servants, not of itself, but of
shareholders.

And, this dilemma is not, as some suppose, tempo-

rary, the aftermath of war, or peculiar to the coal industry, as though the miners alone were the children of
sin which in the last few months they have been described to be. It is permanent; it has spread far; and,
as sleeping spirits are stirred into life by education and
one industry after another develops a strong corporate
consciousness, it will spread further. Nor will it be
resolved by lamentations or menaces or denunciations of
leaders whose only significance is that they say openly
what plain men feel privately. For the matter at bot-
tom is one of psychology. What has happened is that
the motives on which the industrial system relied for
several generations to secure efficiency, secure it no
longer. And it is as impossible to restore them, to
revive by mere exhortation the complex of hopes and
fears and ignorance and patient credulity and passive
acquiescence, which together made men, fifty years
ago, plastic instruments in the hands of industrialism,
as to restore innocence to any others of those who have
eaten of the tree of knowledge.

The ideal of some intelligent and respectable business
men, the restoration of the golden sixties, when workmen
were docile and confiding, and trade unions were still
half illegal, and foreign competition meant English competition in foreign countries, and prices were rising a
little and not rising too much, is the one Utopia which
can never be realized. The King may walk naked as
long as his courtiers protest that he is clad; but when
a child or a fool has broken the spell a tailor is more
important than all their admiration. If the public,
which suffers from the slackening of economic activity,

desires to end its *malaise,* it will not laud as admirable and all-sufficient the operation of motives which are plainly ceasing to move. It will seek to liberate new motives and to enlist them in its service. It will endeavor to find an alternative to incentives which were always degrading, to those who used them as much as to those upon whom they were used, and which now are adequate incentives no longer. And the alternative to the discipline which Capitalism exercised through its instruments of unemployment and starvation is the self-discipline of responsibility and professional pride.

So the demand which aims at stronger organization, fuller responsibility, larger powers for the sake of the producer as a condition of economic liberty, the demand for freedom, is not antithetic to the demand for more effective work and increased output which is being made in the interests of the consumer. It is complementary to it, as the insistence by a body of professional men, whether doctors or university teachers, on the maintenance of their professional independence and dignity against attempts to cheapen the service is not hostile to an efficient service, but, in the long run, a condition of it. The course of wisdom for the consumer would be to hasten, so far as he can, the transition. For, as at present conducted, industry is working against the grain. It is compassing sea and land in its efforts to overcome, by ingenious financial and technical expedients, obstacles which should never have existed. It is trying to produce its results by conquering professional feeling instead of using it. It is carrying not only its inevitable economic burdens, but an ever increasing

load of ill will and skepticism. It has in fact " shot
the bird which caused the wind to blow " and goes about
its business with the corpse round its neck. Compared
with that psychological incubus, the technical deficiencies of industry, serious though they often are, are a
bagatelle, and the business men who preach the gospel
of production without offering any plan for dealing with
what is now the central fact in the economic situation,
resemble a Christian apologist who should avoid disturbing the equanimity of his audience by carefullly
omitting all reference either to the fall of man or the
scheme of salvation. If it is desired to increase the output of wealth, it is not a paradox, but the statement of
an elementary economic truism to say that active and
constructive co-operation on the part of the rank and
file of workers would do more to contribute to that
result than the discovery of a new coal-field or a generation of scientific invention.

The first condition of enlisting on the side of constructive work the professional feeling which is now
apathetic, or even hostile to it, is to secure that when
it is given its results accrue to the public, not to the
owner of property in capital, in land, or in other re-
sources. For this reason the attenuation of the rights
at present involved in the private ownership of industrial capital, or their complete abolition, is not the demand of idealogues, but an indispensable element in a
policy of economic efficiency, since it is the condition of
the most effective functioning of the human beings upon
whom, though, like other truisms, it is often forgotten,

economic efficiency ultimately depends. But it is only one element. Co-operation may range from mere acquiescence to a vigilant and zealous initiative. The criterion of an effective system of administration is that it should succeed in enlisting in the conduct of industry the latent forces of professional pride to which the present industrial order makes little appeal, and which, indeed, Capitalism, in its war upon trade union organization, endeavored for many years to stamp out altogether.

Nor does the efficacy of such an appeal repose upon the assumption of that "change in human nature," which is the triumphant *reductio ad absurdum* advanced by those who are least satisfied with the working of human nature as it is. What it does involve is that certain elementary facts should be taken into account, instead of, as at present, being ignored. That all work is distasteful and that "every man desires to secure the largest income with the least effort" may be as axiomatic as it is assumed to be. But in practice it makes all the difference to the attitude of the individual whether the collective sentiment of the group to which he belongs is on the side of effort or against it, and what standard of effort it sets. That, as employers complain, the public opinion of considerable groups of workers is against an intensification of effort as long as part of its result is increased dividends for shareholders, is no doubt, as far as mere efficiency is concerned, the gravest indictment of the existing industrial order. But, even when public ownership has taken the place of private capitalism, its ability to command effective service will depend ultimately upon its success in securing not merely that professional feeling is no longer an opposing force, but that it is actively enlisted upon the side of maintaining the highest possible standard of efficiency which can reasonably be demanded.

To put the matter concretely, while the existing ownership of mines is a positive inducement to inefficient work, public ownership administered by a bureaucracy, if it would remove the technical deficiencies emphasized by Sir Richard Redmayne as inseparable from the separate administration of 3,000 pits by 1,500 different companies, would be only too likely to miss a capital advantage which a different type of administration would secure. It would lose both the assistance to be derived from the technical knowledge of practical men who know by daily experience the points at which the details of administration can be improved, and the stimulus to efficiency springing from the corporate pride of a profession which is responsible for maintaining and improving the character of its service. Professional spirit is a force like gravitation, which in itself is neither good nor bad, but which the engineer uses, when he can, to do his work for him. If it is foolish to idealize it, it is equally shortsighted to neglect it. In what are described *par excellence* as "the services" it has always been recognized that *esprit de corps* is the foundation of efficiency, and all means, some wise and some mischievous, are used to encourage it: in practice, indeed, the power upon which the country relied as its main safeguard in an emergency was the professional zeal of the navy and nothing else. Nor is that spirit peculiar to the professions which are concerned with war. It is a matter of common training, common responsibilities, and common dangers. In all cases where difficult and disagreeable work is to be done, the force which elicits it is normally not merely money, but the public opinion and tradition of the little society in which the individual moves, and in the esteem of which he finds that which men value in success.

To ignore that most powerful of stimuli as it is ignored to-day, and then to lament that the efforts which it produces are not forthcoming, is the climax of perversity. To aim at eliminating from industry the growth and action of corporate feeling, for fear lest an organized body of producers should exploit the public, is a plausible policy. But it is short-sighted. It is " to pour away the baby with the bath," and to lower the quality of the service in an attempt to safeguard it. A wise system of administration would recognize that professional solidarity can do much of its work for it more effectively than it can do it itself, because the spirit of his profession is part of the individual and not a force outside him, and would make it its object to enlist that temper in the public service. It is only by that policy, indeed, that the elaboration of cumbrous regulations to prevent men doing what they should not, with the incidental result of sometimes preventing them from doing what they should—it is only by that policy that what is mechanical and obstructive in bureaucracy can be averted. For industry cannot run without laws. It must either control itself by professional standards, or it must be controlled by officials who are not of the craft and who, however zealous and well-meaning, can hardly have the feel of it in their fingers. Public control and criticism are indispensable. But they should not be too detailed, or they defeat themselves. It would be better that, once fair standards have been established, the professional organization should check offenses against prices and quality than that it should be necessary for the State to do so. The alternative to minute external supervision is supervision from within by men who become imbued with the public obligations of their trade in the very process of learning it. It is, in short, professional in industry.

For this reason collectivism by itself is too simple a solution. Its failure is likely to be that of other rationalist systems.

> "Dann hat er die Theile in seiner Hand,
>   Fehlt leider! nur das geistige Band."

If industrial reorganization is to be a living reality, and not merely a plan upon paper, its aim must be to secure not only that industry is carried on for the service of the public, but that it shall be carried on with the active co-operation of the organizations of producers. But co-operation involves responsibility, and responsibility involves power. It is idle to expect that men will give their best to any system which they do not trust, or that they will trust any system in the control of which they do not share. Their ability to carry professional obligations depends upon the power which they possess to remove the obstacles which prevent those obligations from being discharged, and upon their willingness, when they possess the power, to use it.

Two causes appear to have hampered the committees which were established in connection with coal mines during the war to increase the output of coal. One was the reluctance of some of them to discharge the invidious task of imposing penalties for absenteeism on their fellow-workmen. The other was the exclusion of faults of management from the control of many committees. In some cases all went well till they demanded that, if the miners were penalized for absenteeism which was due to them, the management should be penalized similarly when men who desired to work were sent home because, as a result of defective organization, there was no work for them to do. Their demand was resisted as "interference with the management," and the attempt to enforce regularity of attendance broke down. Nor, to take another example from the same industry, is it to be expected that the weight of the miners' organization will be thrown on to the side of greater production, if it has no power to insist on the removal of the defects of equipment and organization, the shortage of trams, rails, tubs and timber, the "creaming" of the pits by the working of easily got coal to their future detriment, their wasteful layout caused by the vagaries of separate ownership, by which at present the output is reduced.

The public cannot have it both ways. If it allows workmen to be treated as "hands" it cannot claim the service of their wills and their brains. If it desires them to show the zeal of skilled professionals, it must secure that they have sufficient power to allow of their discharging professional responsibilities. In order that workmen may abolish any restrictions on output which may be imposed by them, they must be able to insist on the abolition of the restrictions, more mischievous because more effective, which, as the Committee on Trusts has recently told us, are imposed by organizations of employers. In order that the miners' leaders, instead of merely bargaining as to wages, hours and working conditions, may be able to appeal to their members to increase the supply of coal, they must be in a position to secure the removal of the causes of low output which are due to the deficiencies of the management, and which are to-day a far more serious obstacle than any reluctance on the part of the miner. If the workmen in the building trade are to take combined action to accelerate production, they must as a body be consulted as to the purpose to which their energy is to be applied, and must not be expected to build fashionable houses, when what are required are six-roomed cottages to house families which are at present living with three persons to a room.

It is deplorable, indeed, that any human beings should consent to degrade themselves by producing the articles which a considerable number of workmen turn out to-day, boots which are partly brown paper, and furniture which is not fit to use. The revenge of outraged humanity is certain, though it is not always obvious; and the penalty paid by the consumer for tolerating an organization of industry which, in the name of efficiency, destroyed the responsibility of the workman, is that the service with which he is provided is not even efficient. He has always paid it, though he has not seen it, in quality. To-day he is beginning to realize that he is likely to pay it in quantity as well. If the public is to get efficient service, it can get it only from human beings, with the initiative and caprices of human beings. It will get it, in short, in so far as it treats industry as a responsible profession.

The collective responsibility of the workers for the maintenance of the standards of their profession is, then, the alternative to the discipline which Capitalism exercised in the past, and which is now breaking down. It involves a fundamental change in the position both of employers and of trade unions. As long as the direction of industry is in the hands of property-owners or their agents, who are concerned to extract from it the maximum profit for themselves, a trade union is necessarily a defensive organization. Absorbed, on the one hand, in the struggle to resist the downward thrust of Capitalism upon the workers' standard of life, and denounced, on the other, if it presumes, to " interfere with management," even when management is most obviously inefficient, it is an opposition which never becomes a government and which has neither the will nor the power to assume responsibility for the quality of the service offered to the consumer. If the abolition of functionless property transferred the control of production to bodies representing those who perform constructive work and those who consume the goods produced, the relation of the worker to the public would no longer be indirect but immediate, and associations which are now purely defensive would be in a position not merely to criticize and oppose but to advise, to initiate and to enforce upon their own members the obligations of the craft.

It is obvious that in such circumstances the service offered the consumer, however carefully safeguarded by his representation on the authorities controlling each industry, would depend primarily upon the success of professional organizations in finding a substitute for the discipline exercised to-day by the agents of property-owners. It would be necessary for them to maintain by their own action the zeal, efficiency and professional pride which, when the barbarous weapons of the nineteenth century have been discarded, would be the only guarantee of a high level of production. Nor, once this new function has been made possible for professional organizations, is there any extravagance in expecting them to perform it with reasonable competence. How far economic motives are balked to-day and could be strengthened by a different type of industrial organization, to what extent, and under what conditions, it is possible to enlist in the services of industry motives which are not purely economic, can be ascertained only after a study of the psychology of work which has not yet been made. Such a study, to be of value, must start by abandoning the conventional assumptions, popularized by economic textbooks and accepted as self-evident by practical men, that the motives to effort are simple and constant in character, like the pressure of steam in a boiler, that they are identical throughout all ranges of economic activity, from the stock exchange to the shunting of wagons or laying of bricks, and that they can be elicited and strengthened only by directly economic incentives. In so far as motives in industry have been considered hitherto, it has usually been done by writers who, like most exponents of scientific management, have started by assuming that the categories of business psychology could be offered with equal success to all classes of workers and to all types of productive work. Those categories appear to be derived from a simplified analysis of the mental processes of the company promoter, financier or investor, and their validity as an interpretation of the motives and habits which determine the attitude to his work of the bricklayer, the miner, the dock laborer or the engineer, is precisely the point in question.

Clearly there are certain types of industry to which they are only partially relevant. It can hardly be assumed, for example, that the degree of skill and energy brought to his work by a surgeon, a scientific investigator, a teacher, a medical officer of health, an Indian civil servant and a peasant proprietor are capable of being expressed precisely and to the same degree in terms of the economic advantage which those different occupations offer. Obviously those who pursue them are influenced to some considerable, though uncertain, extent by economic incentives. Obviously, again, the precise character of each process or step in the exercise of their respective avocations, the performance of an operation, the carrying out of a piece of investigation, the selection of a particular type of educational method, the preparation of a report, the decision of a case or the care of live stock, is not immediately dependent upon an exact calculation of pecuniary gain or loss. What appears to be the case is that in certain walks of life, while the occupation is chosen after a consideration of its economic advantages, and while economic reasons exact the minimum degree of activity needed to avert dismissal from it or "failure," the actual level of energy or proficiency displayed depend largely upon conditions of a different order. Among them are the character of the training received before and after entering the occupation, the customary standard of effort demanded by the public opinion of one's fellows, the desire for the esteem of the small circle in which the individual moves and to be recognized as having "made good" and not to have "failed," interest in one's work, ranging from devotion to a determination to "do justice" to it, the pride of the craftsman, the "tradition of the service."

It would be foolish to suggest that any considerable body of men are uninfluenced by economic considerations. But to represent them as amenable to such incentives only is to give a quite unreal and bookish picture of the actual conditions under which the work of the world is carried on. How large a part such considerations play varies from one occupation to another, according to the character of the work which it does and the manner in which it is organized. In what is called *par excellence* industry, calculations of pecuniary gain and loss are more powerful than in most of the so-called professions, though even in industry they are more constantly present to the minds of the business men who " direct " it, than to those of the managers and technicians, most of whom are paid fixed salaries, or to the rank and file of wage-workers. In the professions of teaching and medicine, in many branches of the public service, the necessary qualities are secured, without the intervention of the capitalist employer, partly by pecuniary incentives, partly by training and education, partly by the acceptance on the part of those entering them of the traditional obligations of their profession as part of the normal framework of their working lives. But this difference is not constant and unalterable. It springs from the manner in which different types of occupation are organized, on the training which they offer, and the *morale* which they cultivate among their members. The psychology of a vocation can in fact be changed; new motives can be elicited, provided steps are taken to allow them free expression. It is as feasible to turn building into an organized profession, with a relatively high code of public honor, as it was to do the same for medicine or teaching.

The truth is that we ought radically to revise the presuppositions as to human motives on which current presentations of economic theory are ordinarily founded and in terms of which the discussion of economic question is usually carried on. The assumption that the stimulus of imminent personal want is either the only spur, or a sufficient spur, to productive effort is a relic of a crude psychology which has little warrant either in past history or in present experience. It derives what plausibility it possesses from a confusion between work in the sense of the lowest *quantum* of activity needed to escape actual starvation, and the work which is given, irrespective of the fact that elementary wants may already have been satisfied, through the natural disposition of ordinary men to maintain, and of extraordinary men to improve upon, the level of exertion accepted as reasonable by the public opinion of the group of which they are members. It is the old difference, forgotten by society as often as it is learned, between the labor of the free man and that of the slave. Economic fear may secure the minimum effort needed to escape economic penalties. What, however, has made progress possible in the past, and what, it may be suggested, matters to the world to-day, is not the bare minimum which is required to avoid actual want, but the capacity of men to bring to bear upon their tasks a degree of energy, which, while it can be stimulated by economic incentives, yields results far in excess of any which are necessary merely to avoid the extremes of hunger or destitution.

That capacity is a matter of training, tradition and habit, at least as much as of pecuniary stimulus, and the ability of a professional association representing the public opinion of a group of workers to raise it is, therefore, considerable. Once industry has been liberated from its subservience to the interests of the functionless property-owner, it is in this sphere that trade unions may be expected increasingly to find their function. Its importance both for the general interests of the community and for the special interests of particular groups of workers can hardly be exaggerated. Technical knowledge and managerial skill are likely to be available as readily for a committee appointed by the workers in an industry as for a committee appointed, as now, by the shareholders. But it is more and more evident to-day that the crux of the economic situation is not the technical deficiencies of industrial organization, but the growing inability of those who direct industry to command the active good will of the *personnel*. Their co-operation is promised by the conversion of industry into a profession serving the public, and promised, as far as can be judged, by that alone.

Nor is the assumption of the new and often disagreeable obligations of internal discipline and public responsibility one which trade unionism can afford, once the change is accomplished, to shirk, however alien they may be to its present traditions. For ultimately, if by slow degrees, power follows the ability to wield it; authority goes with function. The workers cannot have it both ways. They must choose whether to assume the responsibility for industrial discipline and become free, or to repudiate it and continue to be serfs. If, organized as professional bodies, they can provide a more effective service than that which is now, with increasing difficulty, extorted by the agents of capital, they will have made good their hold upon the future. If they cannot, they will remain among the less calculable instruments of production which many of them are to-day. The instinct of mankind warns it against accepting at their face value spiritual demands which cannot justify themselves by practical achievements. And the road along which the organized workers, like any other class, must climb to power, starts from the provision of a more effective economic service than their masters, as their grip upon industry becomes increasingly vacillating and uncertain, are able to supply.

TEN

THE POSITION OF THE BRAIN WORKER

♦

THE conversion of industry into a profession will involve at least as great a change in the position of the management as in that of the manual workers. As each industry is organized for the performance of function, the employer will cease to be a profit maker and become what, in so far as he holds his position by a reputable title, he already is, one workman among others. In some industries, where the manager is a capitalist as well, the alteration may take place through such a limitation of his interest as a capitalist as it has been proposed by employers and workers to introduce into the building industry. In others, where the whole work of administration rests on the shoulders of salaried managers, it has already in part been carried out. The economic conditions of this change have, indeed, been prepared by the separation of ownership from management, and by the growth of an intellectual proletariat to whom the scientific and managerial work of industry is increasingly intrusted. The concentration of businesses, the elaboration of organization, and the developments springing from the application of science to industry have resulted in the multiplication of a body of industrial brain workers who make the old classifications into " employers and workmen," which is still current in common speech, an absurdly misleading description of the industrial system as it exists to-day.

To complete the transformation all that is needed is that this new class of officials, who fifty years ago were almost unknown, should recognize that they, like the manual workers, are the victims of the domination of property, and that both professional pride and economic interest require that they should throw in their lot with the rest of those who are engaged in constructive work. Their position to-day is often, indeed, very far from being a happy one. Many of them, like some mine managers, are miserably paid. Their tenure of their posts is sometimes highly insecure. Their opportunities for promotion may be few, and distributed with a singular capriciousness. They see the prizes of industry awarded by favoritism, or by the nepotism which results in the head of a business unloading upon it a family of sons whom it would be economical to pay to keep out of it, and which, indignantly denounced on the rare occasions on which it occurs in the public service, is so much the rule in private industry that no one even questions its propriety. During the war they have found that, while the organized workers have secured advances, their own salaries have often remained almost stationary, because they have been too genteel to take part in trade unionism, and that to-day they are sometimes paid less than the men for whose work they are supposed to be responsible. Regarded by the workmen as the hangers-on of the masters, and by their employers as one section among the rest of the " hands," they have the odium of capitalism without its power or its profits.

From the conversion of industry into a profession those who at present do its intellectual work have as much to gain as the manual workers. For the principle of function, for which we have pleaded as the basis of industrial organization, supplies the only intelligible standard by which the powers and duties of the different groups engaged in industry can be determined. At the present time no such standard exists. The social order of the pre-industrial era, of which faint traces have survived in the forms of academic organization, was marked by a careful grading of the successive stages in the progress from apprentice to master, each of which was distinguished by clearly defined rights and duties, varying from grade to grade and together forming a hierarchy of functions. The industrial system which developed in the course of the nineteenth century did not admit any principle of organization other than the convenience of the individual, who by enterprise, skill, good fortune, unscrupulous energy or mere nepotism, happened at any moment to be in a position to wield economic authority. His powers were what he could exercise; his rights were what at any time he could assert. The Lancashire mill-owner of the fifties was like the Cyclops, a law unto himself. Hence, since subordination and discipline are indispensable in any complex undertaking, the subordination which emerged in industry was that of servant to master, and the discipline such as economic strength could impose upon economic weakness.

The alternative to the allocation of power by the struggle of individuals for self-aggrandizement is its allocation according to function, that each group in the complex process of production should wield so much authority as, and no more authority than, is needed to enable it to perform the special duties for which it is responsible. An organization of industry based on this principle does not imply the merging of specialized economic functions in an undifferentiated industrial democracy, or the obliteration of the brain workers beneath the sheer mass of artisans and laborers. But it is incompatible with the unlimited exercise of economic power by any class or individual. It would have as its fundamental rule that the only powers which a man can exercise are those conferred upon him in virtue of his office. There would be subordination. But it would be profoundly different from that which exists to-day. For it would not be the subordination of one man to another, but of all men to the purpose for which industry is carried on. There would be authority. But it would not be the authority of the individual who imposes rules in virtue of his economic power for the attainment of his economic advantage. It would be the authority springing from the necessity of combining different duties to attain a common end. There would be discipline. But it would be the discipline involved in pursuing that end, not the discipline enforced upon one man for the convenience or profit of another. Under such an organization of industry the brain worker might expect, as never before, to come to his own. He would be estimated and promoted by his capacity, not by his means. He would be less likely than at present to find doors closed to him because of poverty. His judges would be his colleagues, not an owner of property intent on dividends. He would not suffer from the perversion of values which rates the talent and energy by which wealth is created lower than the possession of property, which is at best their pensioner and at worst the spend-thrift of what intelligence has produced. In a society organized for the encouragement of creative activity those who are esteemed most highly will be those who create, as in a world organized for enjoyment they are those who own.

Such considerations are too general and abstract to carry conviction. Greater concreteness may be given them by comparing the present position of mine-managers with that which they would occupy were effect given to Mr. Justice Sankey's scheme for the nationalization of the Coal Industry. A body of technicians who are weighing the probable effects of such a reorganization will naturally consider them in relation both to their own professional prospects and to the efficiency of the service of which they are the working heads. They will properly take into account questions of salaries, pensions, security of status and promotion. At the same time they will wish to be satisfied as to points which, though not less important, are less easily defined. Under which system, private or public ownership, will they have most personal discretion or authority over the conduct of matters within their professional competence? Under which will they have the best guarantees that their special knowledge will carry due weight, and that, when handling matters of art, they will not be overridden or obstructed by amateurs?

As far as the specific case of the Coal Industry is concerned the question of security and salaries need hardly be discussed. The greatest admirer of the present system would not argue that security of status is among the advantages which it offers to its employees. It is notorious that in some districts, at least, managers are liable to be dismissed, however professionally competent they may be, if they express in public views which are not approved by the directors of their company. Indeed, the criticism which is normally made on the public services, and made not wholly without reason, is that the security which they offer is excessive. On the question of salaries rather more than one-half of the colliery companies of Great Britain themselves supplied figures to the Coal Industry Commission.[1] If their returns may be trusted, it would appear that mine-managers are paid, as a class, salaries the parsimony of which is the more surprising in view of the emphasis laid, and quite properly laid, by the mine-owners on the managers' responsibilities. The service of the State does not normally offer, and ought not to offer, financial prizes comparable with those of private industry. But it is improbable, had the mines been its property during

[1] The Coal Mines Departmenet supplied the following figures to the Coal Industry Commission (Vol. III, App. 66). They relate to 57 per cent. of the colleries of the United Kingdom.

Salary, including bonus and value of house and coal	Number of Manager/ 1913	1919
£100 or less	4	2
£101 to £200	134	3
£201 to £300	280	29
£301 to £400	161	251
£401 to £500	321	213
£501 to £600	57	146
£601 and over	50	152

the last ten years, that more than one-half the managers would have been in receipt of salaries of under £301 per year, and of less than £500 in 1919, by which time prices had more than doubled, and the aggregate profits of the mine-owners (of which the greater part was, however, taken by the State in taxation) had amounted in five years to £160,000,000. It would be misleading to suggest that the salaries paid to mine-managers are typical of private industry, nor need it be denied that the probable effect of turning an industry into a public service would be to reduce the size of the largest prizes at present offered. What is to be expected is that the lower and medium salaries would be raised, and the largest somewhat diminished. It is hardly to be denied, at any rate, that the majority of brain workers in industry have nothing to fear on financial grounds from such a change as is proposed by Mr. Justice Sankey. Under the normal organization of industry, profits, it cannot be too often insisted, do not go to them but to shareholders. There does not appear to be any reason to suppose that the salaries of managers in the mines making more than 5/- profit a ton were any larger than those making under 3/-.

The financial aspect of the change is not, however, the only point which a group of managers or technicians have to consider. They have also to weigh its effect on their professional status. Will they have as much freedom, initiative and authority in the service of the community as under private ownership? How that question is answered depends upon the form given to the administrative system through which a public service is conducted. It is possible to conceive an arrangement under which the life of a mine-manager would be made a burden to him by perpetual recalcitrance on the part of the men at the pit for which he is responsible. It is possible to conceive one under which he would be hampered to the point of paralysis by irritating interference from a bureaucracy at headquarters. In the past some managers of " co-operative workshops " suffered, it would seem, from the former: many officers of Employment Exchanges are the victims, unless common rumor is misleading, of the latter. It is quite legitimate, indeed it is indispensable, that these dangers should be emphasized. The problem of reorganizing industry is, as has been said above, a problem of constitution making. It is likely to be handled successfully only if the defects to which different types of constitutional machinery are likely to be liable are pointed out in advance.

Once, however, these dangers are realized, to devise precautions against them appears to be a comparatively simple matter. If Mr. Justice Sankey's proposals be taken as a concrete example of the position which would be occupied by the managers in a nationalized industry, it will be seen that they do not involve either of the two dangers which are pointed out above. The manager will, it is true, work with a Local Mining Council or pit committee, which is to " meet fortnightly, or oftener if need be, to advise the manager on all questions concerning the direction and safety of the mine," and " if the manager refuses to take the advice of the Local Mining Council on any question concerning the safety and health of the mine, such question shall be referred to the District Mining Council." It is true also that, once such a Local Mining Council is formally established, the manager will find it necessary to win its confidence, to lead by persuasion, not by mere driving, to establish, in short, the same relationships of comradeship and good will as ought to exist between the colleagues in any common undertaking. But in all this there is nothing to undermine his authority, unless "authority" be understood to mean an arbitrary power which no man is fit to exercise, and which few men, in their sober moments, would claim. The manager will be appointed by, and responsible to, not the men whose work he supervises, but the District Mining Council, which controls all the pits in a district, and on that council he will be represented. Nor will he be at the mercy of a distant "clerkocracy," overwhelming him with circulars and overriding his expert knowledge with impracticable mandates devised in London. The very kernel of the schemes advanced both by Justice Sankey and by the Miners' Federation is decentralized administration within the framework of a national system. There is no question of "managing the industry from Whitehall." The characteristics of different coal-fields vary so widely that reliance on local knowledge and experience are essential, and it is to local knowledge and experience that it is proposed to intrust the administration of the industry. The constitution which is recommended is, in short, not "Unitary" but "Federal." There will be a division of functions and power between central authorities and district authorities. The former will lay down general rules as to those matters which must necessarily be dealt with on a national basis. The latter will administer the industry within their own districts, and, as long as they comply with those rules and provide their *quota* of coal, will possess local autonomy and will follow the method of working the pits which they think best suited to local conditions.

Thus interpreted, public ownership does not appear to confront the brain worker with the danger of unintelligent interference with his special technique, of which he is, quite naturally, apprehensive. It offers him, indeed, far larger opportunities of professional development than are open to all but a favored few to-day, when the considerations of productive efficiency, which it is his special *métier* to promote, are liable to be overridden by short-sighted financial interests operating through the pressure of a Board of Directors who desire to show an immediate profit to their shareholders, and who, to obtain it, will " cream " the pit, or work it in a way other than considerations of technical efficiency would dictate. And the interest of the community in securing that the manager's professional skill is liberated for the service of the public, is as great as his own. For the economic developments of the last thirty years have made the managerial and technical *personnel* of industry the repositories of public responsibilities of quite incalculable importance, which, with the best will in the world, they can hardly at present discharge. The most salient characteristic of modern industrial organization is that production is carried on under the general direction of business men, who do not themselves necessarily know anything of productive processes. " Business " and " industry " tend to an increasing extent to form two compartments, which, though united within the same economic system, employ different types of *personnel,* evoke different qualities and recognize different standards of efficiency and workmanship. The technical and managerial staff of industry is, of course, as amenable as other men to economic incentives. But their special work is production, not finance; and, provided they are not smarting under a sense of economic injustice, they want, like most workmen, to " see the job done properly." The business men who ultimately control industry are concerned with the promotion and capitalization of companies, with competitive selling and the advertisement of wares, the control of markets, the securing of special advantages, and the arrangement of pools, combines and monopolies. They are preoccupied, in fact, with financial results, and are interested in the actual making of goods only in so far as financial results accrue from it.

The change in organization which has, to a considerable degree, specialized the spheres of business and management is comparable in its importance to that which separated business and labor a century and a half ago. It is specially momentous for the consumer. As long as the functions of manager, technician and capitalist were combined, as in the classical era of the factory system, in the single person of " the employer," it was not unreasonable to assume that profits and productive efficiency ran similarly together. In such circumstances the ingenuity with which economists proved that, in obedience to " the law of substitution," he would choose the most economical process, machine, or type of organization, wore a certain plausibility. True, the employer might, even so, adulterate his goods or exploit the labor of a helpless class of workers. But as long as the person directing industry was himself primarily a manager, he could hardly have the training, ability or time, even if he had the inclination, to concentrate special attention on financial gains unconnected with, or opposed to, progress in the arts of production, and there was some justification for the conventional picture which represented " the manufacturer " as the guardian of the interests of the consumer. With the drawing apart of the financial and technical departments of industry—with the separation of " business " from " production "—the link which bound profits to productive efficiency is tending to be snapped. There are more ways than formerly of securing the former without achieving the latter; and when it is pleaded that the interests of the captain of industry stimulate the adoption of the most " economical " methods and thus secure industrial progress, it is necessary to ask " economical for whom "? Though the organization of industry which is most efficient, in the sense of offering the consumer the best service at the lowest real cost, may be that which is most profitable to the firm, it is also true that profits are constantly made in ways which have nothing to do with efficient production, and which sometimes, indeed, impede it.

The manner in which " business " may find that the methods which pay itself best are those which a truly scientific " management " would condemn may be illustrated by three examples. In the first place, the whole mass of profits which are obtained by the adroit capitalization of a new business, or the reconstruction of one which already exists, have hardly any connection with production at all. When, for instance, a Lancashire cotton mill capitalized at £100,000 is bought by a London syndicate which re-floats it with a capital of £500,000—not at all an extravagant case—what exactly has happened? In many cases the equipment of the mill for production remains, after the process, what it was before it. It is, however, valued at a different figure, because it is anticipated that the product of the mill will sell at a price which will pay a reasonable profit not only upon the lower, but upon the higher, capitalization. If the apparent state of the market and prospects of the industry are such that the public can be induced to believe this, the promoters of the reconstruction find it worth while to recapitalize the mill on the new basis. They make their profit not as manufacturers, but as financiers. They do not in any way add to the productive efficiency of the firm, but they acquire shares which will entitle them to an increased return. Normally, if the market is favorable, they part with the greater number of them as soon as they are acquired. But, whether they do so or not, what has occurred is a process by which the business element in industry obtains the right to a larger share of the product, without in any way increasing the efficiency of the service which is offered to the consumer.

Other examples of the manner in which the control of

production by "business" cuts across the line of economic progress are the wastes of competitive industry and the profits of monopoly. It is well known that the price paid by the consumer includes marketing costs, which to a varying, but to a large, extent are expenses not of supplying the goods, but of supplying them under conditions involving the expenses of advertisement and competitive distribution. For the individual firm such expenses, which enable it to absorb part of a rival's trade, may be an economy: to the consumer of milk or coal—to take two flagrant instances—they are pure loss. Nor, as is sometimes assumed, are such wastes confined to distribution. Technical reasons are stated by railway managers to make desirable a unification of railway administration and by mining experts of mines. But, up to the war, business considerations maintained the expensive system under which each railway company was operated as a separate system, and still prevent collieries, even collieries in the same district, from being administered as parts of a single organization. Pits are drowned out by water, because companies cannot agree to apportion between them the costs of a common drainage system; materials are bought, and products sold, separately, because collieries will not combine; small coal is left in to the amount of millions of tons because the most economical and technically efficient working of the seams is not necessarily that which yields the largest profit to the business men who control production. In this instance the wide differences in economic strength which exist between different mines discourage the unification which is economically desirable; naturally the directors of a company which owns " a good thing " do not desire to merge interests with a company working coal that is poor in quality or expensive to mine. When, as increasingly happens in other industries, competitive wastes, or some of them, are eliminated by combination, there is a genuine advance in technical efficiency, which must be set to the credit of business motives. In that event, however, the divergence between business interests and those of the consumers is merely pushed one stage further forward; it arises, of course, over the question of prices. If any one is disposed to think that this picture of the economic waste which accompanies the domination of production by business interests is overdrawn, he may be invited to consider the criticisms upon the system passed by the " efficiency engineers," who are increasingly being called upon to advise as to industrial organization and equipment. " The higher officers of the corporation," writes Mr. H. L. Gantt of a Public Utility Company established in America during the war, " have all without exception been men of the ' business ' type of mind, who have made their success through financiering, buying, selling, etc. . . . As a matter of fact it is well known that our industrial system has not measured up as we had expected. . . . *The reason for its falling short is undoubtedly that the men directing it had been trained in a business system operated for profits, and did not understand one operated solely for production.* This is no criticism of the men as individuals; they simply did not know the job, and, what is worse, they did not know that they did not know it."

In so far, then, as "Business" and "Management" are separated, the latter being employed under the direction of the former, it cannot be assumed that the direction of industry is in the hands of persons whose primary concern is productive efficiency. That a considerable degree of efficiency will result incidentally from the pursuit of business profits is not, of course, denied. What seems to be true, however, is that the main interest of those directing an industry which has reached this stage of development is given to financial strategy and the control of markets, because the gains which these activities offer are normally so much larger than those accruing from the mere improvement of the processes of production. It is evident, however, that it is precisely that improvement which is the main interest of the consumer. He may tolerate large profits as long as they are thought to be the symbol of efficient production. But what he is concerned with is the supply of goods, not the value of shares, and when profits appear to be made, not by efficient production, but by skilful financiering or shrewd commercial tactics, they no longer appear meritorious. If, in disgust at what he has learned to call "profiteering," the consumer seeks an alternative to a system under which product is controlled by "Business," he can hardly find it except by making an ally of the managerial and technical *personnel* of industry. They organize the service which he requires; they are relatively little implicated, either by material interest or by psychological bias, in the financial methods which he distrusts; they often find the control of their professions by business men who are primarily financiers irritating in the obstruction which it offers to technical efficiency, as well as sharp and close-fisted in the treatment of salaries. Both on public and professional grounds they belong to a group which ought to take the initiative in promoting a partnership between the producers and the public. They can offer the community the scientific knowledge and specialized ability which is the most important condition of progress in the arts of production. It can offer them a more secure and dignified status, larger opportunities for the exercise of their special talents, and the consciousness that they are giving the best of their work and their lives, not to enriching a handful of uninspiring, if innocuous, share-holders, but to the service of the great body of their fellow-countrymen. If the last advantage be dismissed as a phrase—if medical officers of health, directors of education, directors of the co-operative wholesale be assumed to be quite uninfluenced by any consciousness of social service—the first two, at any rate, remain. And they are considerable.

It is this gradual disengagement of managerial technique from financial interests which would appear the probable line along which " the employer " of the future will develop. The substitution throughout industry of fixed salaries for fluctuating profits would, in itself, deprive his position of half the humiliating atmosphere of predatory enterprise which embarrasses to-day any man of honor who finds himself, when he has been paid for his services, in possession of a surplus for which there is no assignable reason. Nor, once large incomes from profits have been extinguished, need his salary be large,

as incomes are reckoned to-day. It is said that among
the barbarians, where wealth is still measured by cattle,
great chiefs are described as hundred-cow men. The
manager of a great enterprise who is paid £10,000 a
year, might similarly be described as a hundred-family
man, since he receives the income of a hundred families.
It is true that special talent is worth any price, and
that a payment of £10,000 a year to the head of a
business with a turnover of millions is economically a
bagatelle. But economic considerations are not the
only considerations. There is also "the point of
honor." And the truth is that these hundred-family
salaries are ungentlemanly.

When really important issues are at stake every one
realizes that no decent man can stand out for his price.
A general does not haggle with his government for the
precise pecuniary equivalent of his contribution to vic-
tory. A sentry who gives the alarm to a sleeping bat-
talion does not spend next day collecting the capital
value of the lives he has saved; he is paid 1/- a day and
is lucky if he gets it. The commander of a ship does
not cram himself and his belongings into the boats and
leave the crew to scramble out of the wreck as best they
can; by the tradition of the service he is the last man
to leave. There is no reason why the public should
insult manufacturers and men of business by treating
them as though they were more thick-skinned than gen-
erals and more extravagant than privates. To say that
they are worth a good deal more than even the exorbitant salaries which a few of them get is often true.
But it is beside the point. No one has any business to

expect to be paid "what he is worth," for what he is worth is a matter between his own soul and God. What he has a right to demand, and what it concerns his fellow-men to see that he gets, is enough to enable him to perform his work. When industry is organized on a basis of function, that, and no more than that, is what he will be paid. To do the managers of industry justice, this whining for more money is a vice to which they (as distinct from their shareholders) are not particularly prone. There is no reason why they should be. If a man has important work, and enough leisure and income to enable him to do it properly, he is in possession of as much happiness as is good for any of the children of Adam.

ELEVEN

PORRO UNUM NECESSARIUM

♦

So the organization of society on the basis of function, instead of on that of rights, implies three things. It means, first, that proprietary rights shall be maintained when they are accompanied by the performance of service and abolished when they are not. It means, second, that the producers shall stand in a direct relation to the community for whom production is carried on, so that their responsibility to it may be obvious and unmistakable, not lost, as at present, through their immediate subordination to shareholders whose interest is not service but gain. It means, in the third place, that the obligation for the maintenance of the service shall rest upon the professional organization of those who perform it, and that, subject to the supervision and criticism of the consumer, those organizations shall exercise so much voice in the government of industry as may be needed to secure that the obligation is discharged. It is obvious, indeed, that no change of system or machinery can avert those causes of social *malaise* which consist in the egotism, greed, or quarrelsomeness of human nature. What it can do is to create an environment in which those are not the qualities which are encouraged. It cannot secure that men live up to their principles. What it can do is to establish their social order upon principles to which, if they please, they can

live up and not live down. It cannot control their
actions. It can offer them an end on which to fix their
minds. And, as their minds are, so, in the long run
and with exceptions, their practical activity will be.

The first condition of the right organization of industry is, then, the intellectual conversion which, in their
distrust of principles, Englishmen are disposed to place
last or to omit altogether. It is that emphasis should
be transferred from the opportunities which it offers individuals to the social functions which it performs; that
they should be clear as to its end and should judge it
by reference to that end, not by incidental consequences
which are foreign to it, however brilliant or alluring
those consequences may be. What gives its meaning to
any activity which is not purely automatic is its purpose. It is because the purpose of industry, which is
the conquest of nature for the service of man, is neither
adequately expressed in its organization nor present
to the minds of those engaged in it, because it is not
regarded as a function but as an opportunity for personal gain or advancement or display, that the economic
life of modern societies is in a perpetual state of morbid
irritation. If the conditions which produce that unnatural tension are to be removed, it can only be
effected by the growth of a habit of mind which will
approach questions of economic organization from the
standpoint of the purpose which it exists to serve, and
which will apply to it something of the spirit expressed
by Bacon when he said that the work of man ought to
be carried on " for the glory of God and the relief of
men's estate."

Viewed from that angle issues which are insoluble
when treated on the basis of rights may be found more
susceptible of reasonable treatment. For a purpose, is,
in the first place a principle of limitation. It determines the end for which, and therefore the limits within
which, an activity is to be carried on. It divided what
is worth doing from what is not, and settles the scale
upon which what is worth doing ought to be done. It
is in the second place, a principle of unity, because it
supplies a common end to which efforts can be directed,
and submits interests, which would otherwise conflict,
to the judgment of an over-ruling object. It is, in the
third place, a principle of apportionment or distribution. It assigns to the different parties of groups engaged in a common undertaking the place which they
are to occupy in carrying it out. Thus it establishes
order, not upon chance or power, but upon a principle,
and bases remuneration not upon what men can with
good fortune snatch for themselves nor upon what, if
unlucky, they can be induced to accept, but upon what
is appropriate to their function, no more and no less,
so that those who perform no function receive no payment, and those who contribute to the common end receive honourable payment for honourable service.

> Frate, la nostra volontà quieta
> Virtù di carità, che fa volerne
> Sol quel ch'avemo, e d'altro non ci asseta.
> Si disiassimo esse più superne,
> Foran discordi li nostri disiri
> Dal voler di colui che qui ne cerne.

.   .   .   .

Anzi è formale ad esto beato esse
Tenersi dentro alla divina vogli,
Per ch'una fansi nostre vogli e stesse.

.   .   .   .

Chiaro mi fu allor com' ogni dove
In Cielo è paradiso, e sì la grazia
Del sommo ben d'un modo non vi piove.

The famous lines in which Piccarda explains to Dante
the order of Paradise are a description of a complex
and multiform society which is united by overmaster-
ing devotion to a common end. By that end all stations
are assigned and all activities are valued. The parts
derive their quality from their place in the system, and
are so permeated by the unity which they express that
they themselves are glad to be forgotten, as the ribs of
an arch carry the eye from the floor from which they
spring to the vault in which they meet and interlace.

Such a combination of unity and diversity is possible
only to a society which subordinates its activities to
the principle of purpose. For what that principle offers
is not merely a standard for determining the relations
of different classes and groups of producers, but a scale
of moral values. Above all, it assigns to economic activity itself its proper place as the servant, not the
master, of society. The burden of our civilization is
not merely, as many suppose, that the product of industry is ill-distributed, or its conduct tyrannical, or
its operation interrupted by embittered disagreements.
It is that industry itself has come to hold a position of
exclusive predominance among human interests, which
no single interest, and least of all the provision of the

material means of existence, is fit to occupy. Like a
hypochondriac who is so absorbed in the processes of
his own digestion that he goes to his grave before he has
begun to live, industrialized communities neglect the
very objects for which it is worth while to acquire riches
in their feverish preoccupation with the means by which
riches can be acquired.

That obsession by economic issues is as local and
transitory as it is repulsive and disturbing. To future
generations it will appear as pitiable as the obsession
of the seventeenth century by religious quarrels appears
to-day; indeed, it is less rational, since the object with
which it is concerned is less important. And it is a
poison which inflames every wound and turns each
trivial scratch into a malignant ulcer. Society will not
solve the particular problems of industry which afflict
it, until that poison is expelled, and it has learned to
see industry itself in the right perspective. If it is to
do that, it must rearrange its scale of values. It must
regard economic interests as one element in life, not as
the whole of life. It must persuade its members to
renounce the opportunity of gains which accrue without
any corresponding service, because the struggle for them
keeps the whole community in a fever. It must so
organize industry that the instrumental character of
economic activity is emphasized by its subordination to
the social purpose for which it is carried on.

INDEX

Abolition of private ownership, 147

Absenteeism, 152

Absolute rights, 50-51

Absolutism in industry, 144

Acquisitive societies, 29-32

Administration, 115-116

Allocation of power, 163-164

American Constitution, 18-19, 52

Annuities, 74

Arbitration, compulsory, 101

Bacon, quoted, 58, 181

Bentham, 16, 52, 55

Brain workers, position of the, 161-171

British Coal Industry, reorganization of, 166-171

Building Guilds, 103

Building Trade Report, 106-110

Bureaucracy, 116, 149

Capitalism, and production, 173-176; downward thrust of, 154; in America, 101; losing control, 141-142, 148

Cecil, Lord Hugh, 23, 58

Cecil, Robert, 59

Cecil, William, 59

Church and State, 10-13

Coal Industry Commission, 71, 126, 137, 143; report of, 166-167

Coal Mines Committees, 152

Combinations, 125, 130

Committee on Trusts, 153

Competition, 27

Compulsory arbitration, 101

Confiscations, 103

Conservatism, the New, 28

Consumer, exploitation of the, 133-134

Co-operative Movement and cost of coal, 125

Dante, quoted, 182-183

Death Duties, 22

Democratic control, 116

Dickenson, Sir Arthur Lowes, 71

Directorate control, 129

Duckham, Sir Arthur, 119

Duke of Wellington, quoted, 123

Economic confusion, cause of, 131-132

Economic discontent, increase of, 5

Economic egotism, 27,

Economic expansion, 9

Efficiency, the condition of, 139-160; through *Esprit de Corps*, 149-150

Employer, waning power of the, 140

England, and natural right, 15-16; and France contrasted, 16-17; Industrialism in, 44-47; Liberal Movement in, 18; over-crowding of population in, 37; proprietary rights in, 64 *et seq.*

English landlordism, 22-23

Englishmen, characteristics of, 1-3; vanity of, 129

English Revolution of 1688, 52

Esch-Cummins Act, 118

Expediency, rule of, 16

Feudalism, 18

Fixed salaries, 177-178

Forced labor, 102

France, social and industrial conditions in, 16-17; Feudalism in, 18; Revolution in, 15, 65, 69

French Revolution, 15, 65, 69

Function, definition of, 8; as a basis for remuneration, 41-42; as a basis of social reorganization, 180; Function and Freedom, 7

Functional Society, 29, 84-90

Functionless property-owners, 79, 86; abolishment of, 87-88; an expensive luxury, 87

Gainford, Lord, quoted, 26, 111

Gantt, H. L., 175

Government control in war time, 25-26

Ground-rents 89-90, 91

Hobson, Mr., 63

"Hundred-Family Man," 178

Imperial Tobacco Company, 116

Incomes, 41

Income Tax, 22

Income without service, 68

Individualism, 48-49

Individual rights, 9

Individual rights vs. social functions, 27

Industrial problems, 7

Industrial reorganization, 151, 155

Industrial revolution, 9

Industrial societies, 9

Industrial warfare, cause of, and remedy for, 40-42

Industrialism, 18; a poison, 184; compared to Militarism, 44-46; exaggerated estimate of its importance, 45-46; failure of present system, 139-141; nemesis of, 33-51; spread of, 30; tendency of, 31-32

Industry, and a profession, 94, 97; as a profession, 91 et seq., 125-126; deficiencies of, 147; definition of, 6; how private control of may be terminated, 103-104; and the

advantages of such a change, 106; Building Trades' Plan for, 108, 111; motives in, 155-159; nationalization of, 104, 114-118; present organization of intolerable, 129; purpose of, 8, 46, 181; right organization of, 6-7; the means not the end, 46-47

Inheritance taxes, 90

Insurance, 74

Joint control, 111-112

Joint-stock companies, 66

Joint-stock organizations, 97

Labor, absolute rights of, 28; and capital, 98-100, 108; compulsory, 100; control of breaking down, 139 et seq.; degradation of, 35; forced, 102

League of Nations, 101

Liberal Movement, 18

Locke, 14, 52, 55

Management divorced from ownership, 112-113

Mann, Sir John, 126

Militarism, 44-45

Mill, quoted, 89

Mine managers, position of, 162, 166-168

Mining royalties, 23-24, 88

Nationalism, 48-49

Nationalization, 114, 117; of the Coal Industry, 115, 165, 168-169

Natural right in France, 15; in England, 15-16; doctrine of, 21

Officials, position under the present economic system, 162

Old industrial order a failure, 139; its effect on the consumer, 144

Organization, for public service instead of private gains, 127

Over-centralization, 121

Ownership, a new system of, 112-114

Pensioners, 34
Poverty a symptom of social disorder, 5
Private enterprise and public ownership, 118-120
Private ownership, 120; abolition of, 147; of industrial capital, 105-106
Private rights and public welfare, 14-15
Privileges, 24
Producer, obligation of the, 127-128; responsibility of, 128
Production, increased, 5; large scale and small scale, 87; misdirection of, 37-39; why not increased, 136
Productivity, 4, 46
Professional Spirit, the, 149-150
Profits, and production, 173-176; division of, 133
Proletariat, 19, 65
Property, absolute rights of, 52, 80; and creative work, 52 et seq.; classification of, 63, 64; complexity of, 75; functionless, 76-77, 81; in land, 56-60; in rights and royalties, 62; minority ownership of, 79; most ambiguous of categories, 53-54; passive ownership of, 62; private, 70-72; protection of, 78-79; rights, 50-51; security in, 72-73; socialist fallacy regarding, 86
Proudhon, 54
Publicity of costs and profits, 85, 123-124, 126, 132

Redmayne, Sir Richard, 149
Reformation the, 10-13; effect on society, 12-14
Reform Bill of 1832, 69
Religion, 10; changes in, 11-12
Report of the United States Industrial Commission, 1916, 128-129
Riches, meaning of, 98
Rights of Man, French Declaration of, the, 16, 52
Rights, and Functions, 8-19; doctrine of, 21 et seq, 43-44; without functions, 61
Rights of the shareholder, 75
Royalties, 23-24, 62
Royalties, and property, 70; from coal mining properties, 88; a tax upon the industry of others, 89

Sankey, Justice, 115, 117, 143, 165, 167, 168, 169
Security of income, 73-75
Service as a basis of remuneration, 25, 41-42, 85, 133
Shareholders, 91-92
Shells, cost of making, 124-125
Smith, Adam, 15, 52, 95
Social inequality, 36-37
Social reorganizations, schemes for, 5
Social war, 40
Socialism, 53
Society, duality of modern, 135
Society, functional organization of, 52
State management, 116, 117
Steel Corporation, 116
Supervision from within, 151
Syndicalism, 130

Taxation, 22
Trusts, Report on, 23

United States, transformation in, 65
Utilitarians, the English, 17
Utility, 16-17

"Vicious Circle," the, 43, 123-138
Voltaire, quoted, 55

Wages and costs, 131
Wages and profits, 78
Wealth, acquisition of, 20 et

seq.; as foundation for public esteem, 35-36; distribution of on basis of function, 77; fallacy of increased, 42-45; how to increase output of, 147; inequality of, 37-38; limitation of, 36-37; output of, 37-38; production and consumption of—a contrast, 77-78; waste of, 37-39

Whitley Councils, 110

Women self-supporting, 74

Worker and Spender, 77-78

Workers, collective responsibility of, 154

Workers' control, 128

Workmen, as "hands," 152; present independence of, 145-146; responsibility of destroyed, 153-154; servants of shareholders, 136-137; treatment of, 152-153